Shortcuts

FOR

TEACHING READING COMPREHENSION

Cover by Janet Skiles

Copyright © Good Apple, Inc., 1990

ISBN No. 0-86653-515-2

Printing No. 987654321

Good Apple, Inc.
Box 299
Carthage, IL 62321-0299

By Flora Joy

Illustrated by Pat Harroll

Teaching comprehension can be fun!

GA1144

TABLE OF CONTENTS

Introduction

Part 1

Part 2

This book is divided into two parts:

Part 1 presents nine areas of comprehension subskills to be considered by all teachers of reading. The information in this section blends with any currently existing method of reading instruction.

Part 2 demonstrates how the textual material in Part 1 may be practically applied in a classroom or tutorial situation.

GA1144

SHORTCUTS FOR TEACHING READING

COMPREHENSION

AN INTRODUCTION

The material offered in this book is intended to complement and supplement **any** existing reading program used in the classroom or home. These activities provide support and extension exercises for all current basal approaches and natural language methods of learning.

Although the structure of this text begins with separate (but overlapping) comprehension skills, the intention is only to offer an organized method of dealing with the numerous tasks in comprehension rather than to suggest that comprehension is a collection of *separable* units. No researcher has ever determined just exactly what happens when a student reads a selection and attempts to comprehend the passage. No one can "open the brain" and see how all the mental processes are functioning as one reads. What **is known**, however, is that students can be encouraged to cope better with the global comprehension tasks if stimulating and challenging questions are prepared and presented.

Quite frequently teachers or parents with no training or practice in the preparation of comprehension questions resort to the "facts only" types of questions, such as "In what year was the War of 1812?" or "How many freckles were on George Washington's left cheek?" or "In what city was the Philadelphia chromosome discovered?"

This type of experience, especially if repeated year after year in the classroom, trains students to learn the facts only (and often the insignificant ones) to repeat on a test or work sheet. This process seldom, if ever, encourages the development of the higher level thinking skills. **With training and practice,** however, all instructional leaders can engage in classroom activities which both promote the higher level thinking skills **and** which are challenging and fun for the learners.

This book has three goals which are explained below.

GOAL 1

The first goal is to encourage instructional leaders who have engaged in the "fact only" types of comprehension questions to examine a more creative type of material. The intended outcome of this goal is to produce learners who become more excited about dealing with the comprehension process.

GOAL 2

The second goal is for the instructional leader to **extend** the materials provided in this book. This may be done by examining each future reading selection to be presented to a group of learners and adapting the provided suggested ideas in this document to fit the passage to be used.

GA1144

GOAL 3

The third goal is for the learners to become individuals **who WANT to read** rather than students who read only **when forced to do so** by the current educational system. This last goal is by far the most important of the three. All too frequently today's students perform only at the minimum levels because they *do not enjoy* that which they are required to read. If these learners are given exciting and challenging materials (frequently without a numerical "grade"), then perhaps their responses to the learning process will lean more in the positive direction.

In order to accomplish the above goals, the material in this book is offered in two parts.

PART 1

The first section introduces and explains several basic comprehension skills which have been described by reading researchers as needing to be taught in the early grades. Although these skills are explained separately, they are frequently combined in the various questioning tasks in the classroom.

The skills presented are as follows:

SEQUENCE

Determining the **MAIN IDEA**

Determining **CHARACTER** Traits or Personality Descriptions

Determining what is **REAL OR UN-REAL** and what is Fact or Opinion

Noting **DETAILS**

PREDICTION or Projection

Understanding **WORDS OR PHRASES**

Additional skills of **INFERENCE**

and

READER REACTION, Response, and Judgment

For each of the above skills a general explanation is given, followed by numerous exercises, activities, and suggestions for continuing the skills. Several reproducible pages are provided. All of the materials may be reused as often as desired. It is suggested that the purchaser of this book save these pages as originals and continue to photocopy any of the pages as often as desired.

PART 2

After a multitude of exercises and activities offered for the general comprehension subskills, one specific story is included and followed by a set of comprehension activities for that story only.

Any story could be prepared in this same fashion. "The Wolf and the Seven Little Goats" is provided as an example.

Following the presentations of both Parts 1 and 2, selected students may attempt the writing of comprehension questions for a designated story. This writing task is very challenging indeed and offers a special and unique type of learning experience.

Some of the provided activities and exercises are not designed for *a numerical grade.* This is intentional! Not all educational experiences should result in a "92" as an evaluative response by an instructional leader. For those instances when numerical grades are mandatory, consider giving "100" for those who have demonstrated maximum effort! The key to any comprehension activity is for the student to en**JOY** the learning process. Always keep this goal in sight!

Part 1

GA1144

INSTRUCTIONAL OBJECTIVES FOR PART 1

For those educational settings desiring or requiring written instructional objectives for each activity, the following may be used for the pages in Part 1. Since many variations of these activities exist, these stated objectives may be reworded to fit any instructional need.

Pages 13-22: The learner will accurately draw lines (straight and/or curved) to depict the order of events in a story.

Pages 25-30: The learner will accurately arrange sets of two, three, or four pictures in a logical sequential order.

Pages 35-42: The learner will accurately arrange sets of pictures and/or words (which correspond to a popular children's story) in a logical sequential order.

Pages 47-56: The learner will accurately arrange sets of word groups in a logical sequential order.

Pages 66-69: The learner will accurately select a provided title which corresponds to a main thought depicted via a picture.

Pages 70-73: The learner will accurately select a provided picture which reflects the main thought of a reading passage. (Answers for this section are: Elephant = 2, Count = 1, Monster = 4, and Cats = 3.)

Pages 74-75: The learner will accurately select a provided title which reflects the main thought of a printed passage. (Answers for this section are: Anteater = D, Giraffes = C, Hair = A, and Elephants = B.)

Pages 76-80: The learner will create an appropriate main idea statement for an identified passage and write it on a provided visual.

Pages 85-87: The learner will select an appropriate picture which corresponds to an identified character at a specified point in a reading selection.

Pages 88-90: The learner will select an appropriate vocabulary term which matches an identified pictorial representation of a character.

Pages 88-90: The learner will select an appropriate character trait card which matches an identified character at a specified point in a reading selection.

Page 94: The learner will accurately determine whether a drawing is that of a real animal or an animal which is protrayed in fantasy form.

Page 97: The learner will provide a logical outcome for a predictable scene.

Page 98: The learner will provide a logical verbal response for an indicated character in a cartoon setting.

Pages 103-106: The learner will demonstrate knowledge of picture interpretation by appropriately responding to both literal and inferential detail questions corresponding to the picture.

Pages 107-110: The learner will demonstrate knowledge of picture and passage interpretation by determining the differences in the details of the two.

Pages 114-116: The learner will demonstrate knowledge of the higher-level cognitive (thinking) skills by interpreting the humor reflected in provided cartoons.

Page 118 and 120: The learner will accurately reflect his/her own feelings or judgments by selecting a corresponding response card which matches this emotion.

Pages 121-122: The learner will make an opinionated judgment based on provided information regarding the traits of a selected character by selecting (or preparing) a corresponding character badge.

Pages 123-124: The learner will verbalize his/her feelings regarding the major thoughts or happenings in a reading passage by stating them on prepared "signs."

GA1144

TEACHING THE COMPREHENSION SUBSKILL OF

The comprehension subskill of sequence involves the reader's arranging the events described in a passage in an appropriate order. A task which does not require this of the reader is **not a sequence** task. This specific comprehension skill has been found to be relatively difficult for many students—depending, of course, upon the style and complexity. Much attention is given to words such as **next, before, first, second, at last,** etc.

To introduce the skill of sequence to a classroom, ask learners to list the steps necessary for making a peanut butter sandwich. Write these steps as the students volunteer them. Then take a jar of peanut butter (and bread, etc.) and try to follow these dictated steps. This will frequently be humorous since few students remember to offer steps such as "Take the lid off the jar," or "Open the loaf of bread (or crackers)."

Sequence questions may be prepared in many different ways and they may have a wide range of difficulty for the learner. The following pages provide some examples and general information regarding the preparation and use of sequence questions.

SAMPLE QUESTION STYLES

STYLE A: LINE DESIGN

Young readers facing initial on-paper comprehension tasks need to begin with those involving easier and limited procedures. The line design style of question asks the reader to think about the content of the passage, then (at an indicated starting point) to **draw lines** indicating the sequence of events of that selection. The lines drawn by the reader reflect that reader's comprehension of that passage. Pages 11-22 provide further explanation and samples of this style.

STYLE B: PICTURE MANIPULATIVES

The majority of young readers prefer to manipulate items for learning rather than to write answers on a work sheet. Picture manipulatives, therefore, provide a question style which may greatly reinforce the comprehension skill of sequence. See pages 23-32 for further explanation and several samples of this style.

STYLE C: PICTURE/PASSAGE MANIPULATIVES

This style combines the information which may be interpreted from simple drawings with information from words only. A variety of materials may be prepared, as shown and explained on pages 33-44.

STYLE D: PASSAGE MANIPULATIVES

After learners have gained experience with logical arrangement of events through pictures,

GA1144

then information through words only may be used to continue the development of this skill. Pages 45-56 provide further explanation and samples of this style.

STYLE E: WRITTEN QUESTIONS

A variety of written questions may be used to build the skill of sequence. Pages 57-60 provide further explanation and samples of some written questions.

SEQUENCE LEARNING CENTERS

A learning center on the comprehension skill of sequence may be prepared which displays all of the material in this section. Below is a pictorial representation of such a center.

SEQUENCE SECTION A: LINE DESIGN ACTIVITIES

One method of allowing young learners to indicate their knowledge of the **order of events** in the selection they have just read or heard is to **draw lines** indicating such a sequence. This style involves a brief reading passage and a picture revealing all of the possible actions in the passage. The reading selection may either be kept in view (for reference) or it may be removed. After encountering the passage, the learner will draw a line in the picture (beginning at an indicated starting point) to show all of the actions in the story in the order in which they occurred.

The materials on the following pages may be used as samples of this type of sequence activity. These samples intentionally cover a wide range of abilities. The first one requires a simple two-step drawing. This is a suggested starter to introduce the activity. As learners are able, they may proceed to the last activity which requires a multi-step drawing.

There are several ways these pages may be prepared.

1. The activity page (story and design) may be photocopied for each student. These students may draw the sequence of events with their regular pencils or markers. They may check their drawings with the provided answer key. (This answer key may be photocopied from this text and prepared in a *permanent reusable fashion* to be kept by the instructor.) Learners may color the design after they have completed the activity. These sheets may be discarded and new ones photocopied for each new individual or group.

2. For permanent reusable student copies,

The Two Dogs

Ruff wanted to find Sparky.
He looked in Sparky's house.
He looked near Sparky's food dish.
There he found Sparky.
Sparky was asleep.

Read to the student: Place your pencil on the picture of Ruff.
Draw a line to show where he went to find Sparky.

Tim, the Fish

Tim is a small fish.
He swam under the shark.
He swam over the rock.
He swam to the shell.
He ate the bait on the hook.

Read to the student: Place your pencil on the picture of Tim.
Draw a line to show all of the places he swam.

GA1144

the sample pages may be carefully cut from the text. Each page (front with story and design, back with answers) may be laminated or covered with a clear self-adhesive paper. These pages may be given to learners to work. Learners may mark on them with a grease pencil (or other easily erased marker). After the learners draw the lines indicating the sequence of the story, they may turn the page over to check their answers. (This same procedure may occur with photocopies instead of the actual pages from this text. In this manner, an original copy is always available to be recopied in case of loss, damage, etc.)

3. For a format similar to that described in the above step, a colored file folder may be used. The story and design may appear on the front of the file folder. The answer key may be hidden inside. (Both pages are laminated or covered with clear self-adhesive paper.) Students can mark on the top part of the file folder, then they would check their answers by opening the folder.

4. Transparencies may be made of the page containing the story and design. The instructor could read the story aloud and volunteer students could orally indicate where the lines should be drawn. A grease pencil could be used to mark on the transparency film. These marks are easily removed with a paper towel. In this fashion the activity could be a cooperative group experience.

Additional designs may be prepared for this style by sketching the "floor plan" of the action in a selected passage and letting the students trace the sequence of events. For example, a selection in a basal reader which has much action might lend itself to this style of activity. Either the instructor or talented students may provide the drawing. This may be drawn on regular paper, or the chalkboard may be used. The chalkboard experience might involve having the students volunteer what the story "floor plan" might be as one student (or instructor) draws the design. A multitude of possibilities exists for such drawings.

The Two Dogs

Ruff wanted to find Sparky.
He looked in Sparky's house.
He looked near Sparky's food dish.
There he found Sparky.
Sparky was asleep.

Read to the student: Place your pencil on the picture of Ruff.
Draw a line to show where he went to find Sparky.

SPARKY

SPARKY

13

ANSWER:

The Two Dogs

Ruff wanted to find Sparky.
He looked in Sparky's house.
He looked near Sparky's food dish.
There he found Sparky.
Sparky was asleep.

*Read to the student: Place your pencil on the picture of Ruff.
Draw a line to show where he went to find Sparky.*

14

Tim, the Fish

Tim is a small fish.
He swam under the shark.
He swam over the rock.
He swam to the shell.
He ate the bait on the hook.

*Read to the student: Place your pencil on the picture of Tim.
Draw a line to show all of the places he swam.*

15

GA1144

ANSWER:

Tim, the Fish

Tim is a small fish.
He swam under the shark.
He swam over the rock.
He swam to the shell.
He ate the bait on the hook.

Read to the student: Place your pencil on the picture of Tim.
Draw a line to show all of the places he swam.

16

Katy's Mitten

Katy Kitten lost her mitten. Where could it be? She looked under the big chair. It was not there.

She looked under the television set. She did not see it. She jumped to the top of the table. She could not find it.

She walked to the closet door, but she could not go inside. On the floor by the closet was a shoe. She looked inside it. She saw no mitten. So she went back to her box.

She looked at her paw. Then she saw her mitten. It had been on her paw all along!

Read to the student: Place your pencil on the words "Start here."
Draw a line to show all of the places Katy looked for her mitten.
Draw them in the order in which she looked for them.

× Start here.

GA1144

ANSWER:

Katy's Mitten

Katy Kitten lost her mitten. Where could it be? She looked under the big chair. It was not there.

She looked under the television set. She did not see it. She jumped to the top of the table. She could not find it.

She walked to the closet door, but she could not go inside. On the floor by the closet was a shoe. She looked inside it. She saw no mitten. So she went back to her box.

She looked at her paw. Then she saw her mitten. It had been on her paw all along!

Read to the student: Place your pencil on the words "Start here."
Draw a line to show all of the places Katy looked for her mitten.
Draw them in the order in which she looked for them.

× Start here.

18

GA1144

Burt's Party

Burt Beaver wanted to have an animal party. He wrote letters to his animal friends. He took the letters by their homes and placed them in their mailboxes.

First he went to Sam Squirrel's house. He placed a letter in Sam's box.

Then he went to Charlotte Chipmunk's home. He also put a letter in her mailbox. He did the same for Freddy Frog and Sandra Snake.

On his way back home he put a letter in Mary Mouse's box. Then he looked in his own mailbox. There was a nice letter from a friend. It made him feel good.

Read to the students: Place your pencil on Burt Beaver's home. Draw a line to each mailbox which he touched. Draw these in order.

GA1144

ANSWER:

Burt's Party

Burt Beaver wanted to have an animal party. He wrote letters to his animal friends. He took the letters by their homes and placed them in their mailboxes.

First he went to Sam Squirrel's house. He placed a letter in Sam's box.

Then he went to Charlotte Chipmunk's home. He also put a letter in her mailbox. He did the same for Freddy Frog and Sandra Snake.

On his way back home he put a letter in Mary Mouse's box. Then he looked in his own mailbox. There was a nice letter from a friend. It made him feel good.

Read to the students: Place your pencil on Burt Beaver's home. Draw a line to each mailbox which he touched. Draw these in order.

GA1144

Harry's Trip

Early one day Harry Hare climbed into his Rabbit Rocket Ship. He flew to Carrot City to visit his brother. Carrot City was always covered with carrots. Harry liked carrots. Harry and his brother ate carrots and played all morning.

Harry returned to his Rabbit Rocket Ship and flew to Cabbage Cove. His sister lived there. They ate cabbages and played.

Later he flew to Lettuce Falls. He was too stuffed to eat any more. So he flew to the Toy Town to buy some new toys.

Next he went to Snow Hills to slide down the hill in the snow. He then went to Crooked Creek for a tasty drink of cool water.

It had been a long day. Harry Hare was tired. For the last time he climbed into his Rabbit Rocket Ship. He flew home. That night he slept soundly and had good dreams.

Student directions: Place your pencil on the Rabbit Rocket Ship. Draw a line to show all of the places (in order) to which Harry flew during this story. Be sure to keep them in order.

GA1144

ANSWER:

Harry's Trip

Early one day Harry Hare climbed into his Rabbit Rocket Ship. He flew to Carrot City to visit his brother. Carrot City was always covered with carrots. Harry liked carrots. Harry and his brother ate carrots and played all morning.

Harry returned to his Rabbit Rocket Ship and flew to Cabbage Cove. His sister lived there. They ate cabbages and played.

Later he flew to Lettuce Falls. He was too stuffed to eat any more. So he flew to the Toy Town to buy some new toys.

Next he went to Snow Hills to slide down the hill in the snow. He then went to Crooked Creek for a tasty drink of cool water.

It had been a long day. Harry Hare was tired. For the last time he climbed into his Rabbit Rocket Ship. He flew home. That night he slept soundly and had good dreams.

Student directions: Place your pencil on the Rabbit Rocket Ship. Draw a line to show all of the places (in order) to which Harry flew during this story. Be sure to keep them in order.

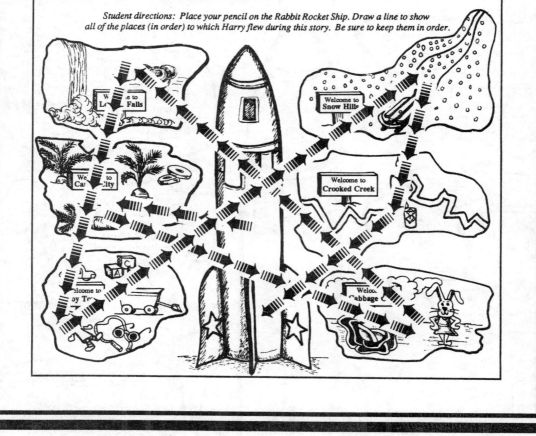

GA1144

SEQUENCE SECTION B: PICTURE MANIPULATIVES

One method for learners to indicate their knowledge of the order of events in a selection is for them to **arrange related pictures in a logical order.** It is generally easier for young learners if these pictures are **separate moveable items** which may be positioned and repositioned than if these same pictures are to be numbered on one intact sheet. Many young learners have not developed sufficient mental maturity to determine a logical order of pictures which cannot **actually be moved about** for examination and reexamination.

PREPARING PROVIDED SAMPLES

Pages 25-30 may be photocopied and used as starter samples for this style of sequence question. Three different levels of difficulty appear on these pages. For the **very young** learner who is just beginning the understanding of both the sequence of events and the use of manipulatives, use page 25. This page contains pictures with only two frames per set. After learners master the placing of **two** pictures in a logical order, continue with page 27 (**three** frames per envelope), then to page 29 (**four** frames per envelope).

These sample pages may be prepared by carefully removing the sheets at the dotted lines. Numerical answers automatically appear on the backs of the pages. The sheets may be laminated or covered with clear self-adhesive paper. (By so doing, the activity may be reused hundreds of times by young learners.) The individual frames in each separate set should be cut out and placed into a small envelope or a library card pocket **in mixed order.** Each envelope should be labeled with the set number. In this fashion stray pieces may be returned to the right place without reexamining all sets.

PREPARING ADDITIONAL SETS

Several additional sets may be prepared in one of two ways.

1. The blank shapes on pages 31 and 32 may be photocopied and given to learners. They may think of new possible picture sequences to draw for others to place in order.

These possibilities are endless and fun for most learners. (It is suggested that little attention be paid to the quality of the art and much attention be given to the thought behind the picture sequence.)

GA1144

2. Newspaper comic strips provide a steady and reliable source for this type of teaching material. Caution should be exercised, however, in the selection of such comic strips. First, not all comic strips which appear in daily newspapers are understood by **young** learners. Frequently, the thought sequence requires adult maturity to determine the appropriate order of events. Second, several understandable comic strips have **interchangeable** frames. These items, although appropriate for younger students, could not be used for **sequencing** skills because **several** logical arrangements of the individual cartoon frames might be considered appropriate. However, it is feasible to omit some of the frames if such omission could create useable materials.

For these newspaper comic strips to be **self-checking** materials, the answers may be placed on the backs of the individually cut frames. Several levels of difficulty of self-correcting materials may be considered. The easiest level is to write or type **numerals** on the backs of the frames (as has been done with the provided samples in this text). **Letters** of the alphabet may also be used. A harder method (only for readers and spellers) is to arrange the letters on the backs of the frames so they **spell a word** when placed in the appropriate order and turned over one at a time. Make sure the learners can spell simple words before selecting this method. Caution is given not to select words with repeated letters (such as **meet** or **add**) or words which may be rearranged to form other words (such as **read** and **dear**). A sample word for a four-frame sequence is **pond**. The letter **p** is written on the back of the first frame in the sequence. The letter **o** is written on the back of the second frame, the letter **n** on the back of the third, and the letter **d** on the back of the last. By using this method, students are not at an advantage if they "peep" (accidentally, of course) at the back of a card while removing them from the envelopes.

To prepare these materials for **permanent use** by students, first photocopy the desired cartoon strips. Write the answers on the backs of each separate item. (Be careful not to use markers which *bleed through* the paper.) Laminate all pages (or cover with clear self-adhesive paper). Carefully cut into separate pieces. Place all pieces **for each separate set** IN MIXED ORDER into one envelope or library card pocket. Label that envelope by the set number (and write this same set number on each enclosed separate frame). Also place on the outside of the envelope the number of items which **should be** included in the set. By so doing, any stray pieces may be easily returned to the appropriate container. This also helps to determine when a frame has been lost.

For **unphotocopied** newspaper cartoon strips, cover the fronts of the materials with clear self-adhesive paper and the backs with solid or decorative self-adhesive paper. This will omit the confusion of seeing whatever appeared in the newspaper on the *backs* of the selected cartoon strips. Write the answers on the backs with permanent markers.

This style has a multitude of additional possibilities of picture content. For example, some magazine ads frequently provide interesting and challenging pictures for students to use. Carefully search through brochures and what is typically called "junk mail" for possible picture sequences. It is amazing what can be collected and prepared as interesting classroom teaching materials!

GA1144

Set 1

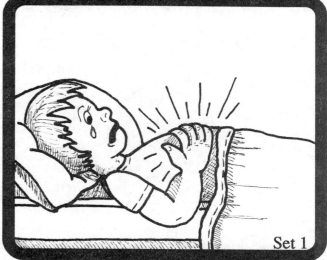

Set 1

Set 2

Set 2

Set 3

Set 3

GA1144

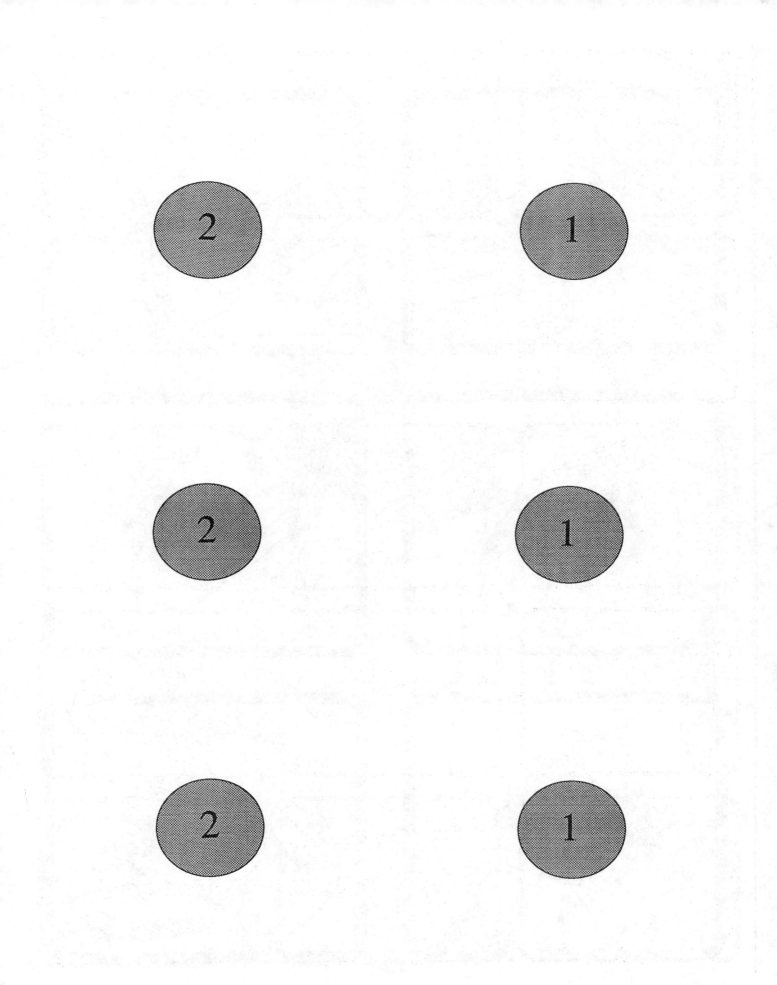

GA1144

GA1144

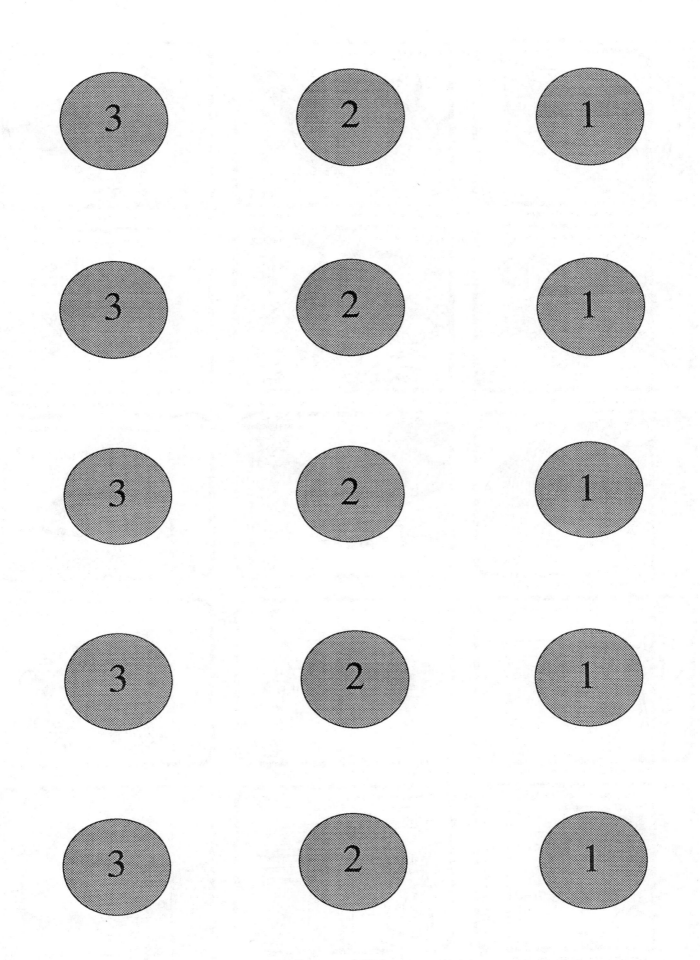

28

GA1144

29

GA1144

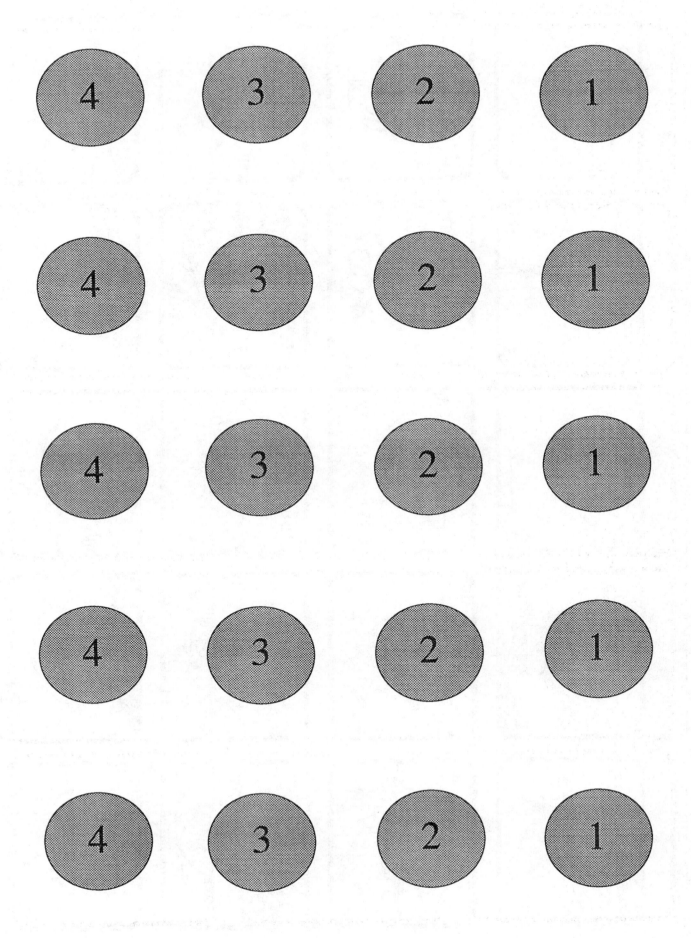

30

Blank frames for preparing additional sequence sets (3 per set)

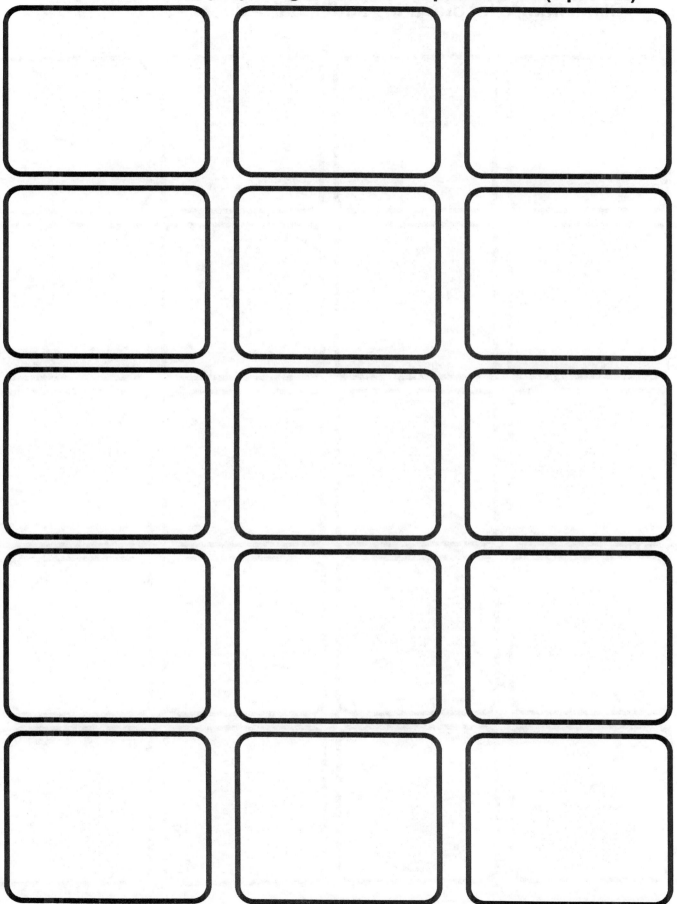

31

GA1144

Blank frames for preparing additional sequence sets (4 per set)

GA1144

SEQUENCE SECTION C: PICTURE/PASSAGE MANIPULATIVES

For a more difficult activity than those described in Section B, materials may include **both** pictures and printed paragraphs. Both these pictures and word groups may be arranged in order, either separately or as an entire group.

The actual **preparation** of such materials will be similar to that described in first part of Section B.

Pages 35-42 may be photocopied and used for this style. Note that the rewritten (and redrawn) versions of these childhood stories are *not intended* to be either complete or literary. Some of the versions are intentionally different from the standard stories in order to **force** the thinking through of a logical order of events. All are prepared solely for the purpose of providing a variety of sequencing activities for young learners. A variety of finished formats

may be considered. Below are some suggestions.

Folder Style 1: This style leaves the word frames intact and pasted inside a folder (or onto a large stiff piece of paper). An envelope houses the individually cut frames which are to be placed onto numbered rectangles beside the corresponding word frames. In this manner non-readers may participate in the activity simply by placing the pictures in order. As they gain maturity in the reading skills, the corresponding paragraphs may be read and studied.

Folder Style 2: This style leaves the pictures intact and pasted inside a folder. The accompanying envelope houses the word frames which are to be placed onto numbered and lettered frames beside their corresponding pictures.

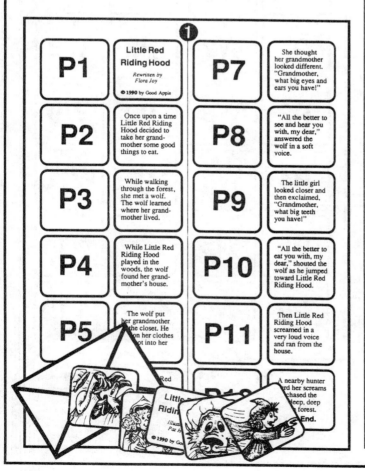

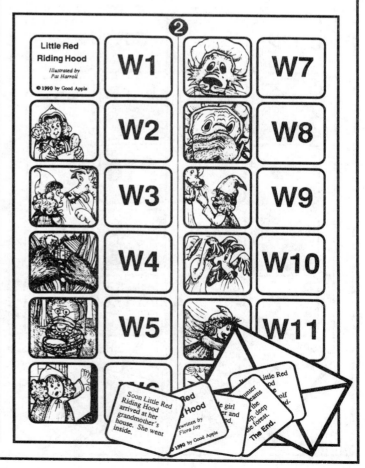

GA1144

Folder Style 3: This style leaves each alternating picture and word frame intact and pasted inside a folder. The accompanying envelope houses the remaining frames which are to be matched with their corresponding frame on the folder.

Folder Style 4: This style has **all** frames cut out to be placed onto corresponding picture and word rectangles inside a folder.

In the preparation of any of the above styles, note that *The Three Little Pigs* is twice the length of the other provided samples. With folder use this will involve two pages pasted on the insides of an open folder.

Other variations of the above arrangements exist. For example, using *no folders at all* and having learners arrange the word frames and pictures on a blank tabletop is acceptable. Any style which fits the needs of the learners should be considered.

After completing the samples provided in this text, learners may prepare additional examples if they wish. Page 43 may be photocopied and given to those who are interested. Using all of the frames on this page will not be necessary; nor should learners be restricted to those provided on this sheet.

Special note: Page 44 of this text may be photocopied and placed inside a file folder to assist in the preparation of these four described styles. Simply paste this photocopy on the inside of the folder. Atop the corresponding frames, paste any frames which are to be left permanently inside the folder. The remaining frames are cut out separately and placed in envelopes. Note that the letter **W** *indicates that a word frame is needed and the letter* **P** *requests the pictures.*

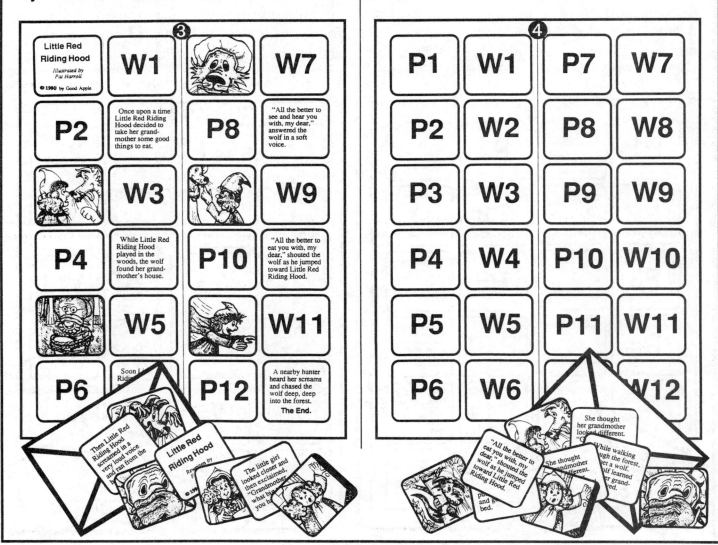

GA1144

Little Red Riding Hood

*Illustrated by
Pat Harroll*

Little Red Riding Hood

*Rewritten by
Flora Joy*

Once upon a time Little Red Riding Hood decided to take her grandmother some good things to eat.

While walking through the forest, she met a wolf. The wolf learned where her grandmother lived.

While Little Red Riding Hood played in the woods, the wolf found her grandmother's house.

The wolf put her grandmother in the closet. He put on her clothes and got into her bed.

Soon Little Red Riding Hood arrived at her grandmother's house. She went inside.

She thought her grandmother looked different. "Grandmother, what big eyes and ears you have!"

"All the better to see and hear you with, my dear," answered the wolf in a soft voice.

The little girl looked closer and then exclaimed, "Grandmother, what big teeth you have!"

"All the better to eat you with, my dear," shouted the wolf as he jumped toward Little Red Riding Hood.

Then Little Red Riding Hood screamed in a very loud voice and ran from the house.

A nearby hunter heard her screams and chased the wolf deep, deep into the forest.

The End.

GA1144

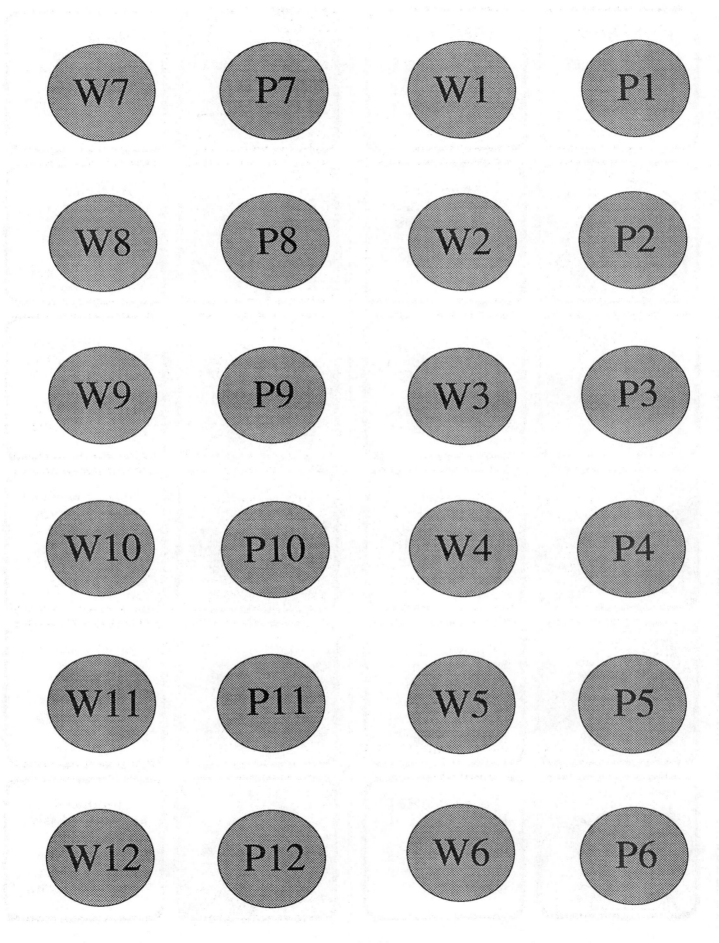

36

GA1144

The Three Bears

Illustrated by Pat Harroll

© 1990 by Good Apple

The Three Bears

Rewritten by Flora Joy

© 1990 by Good Apple

Once upon a time there were three bears. There was Papa Bear, Mama Bear, and Baby Bear.

One day the three bears went for a walk in the woods. While they were gone, Goldilocks came walking by.

She went inside and saw three bowls of porridge sitting on the kitchen table.

She tasted the big one. It was too hot. The next one was too cold. The tiny one was just right, so she ate it all up.

Then she sat in a big chair, but it was too hard. She sat in another chair that was too soft.

Then she sat in a tiny chair. It felt just right. But as she sat in it, it broke into many pieces!

Goldilocks went into the bedroom. She lay on a big bed. It was too hard. The middle-sized bed was too soft.

Then she lay on the tiny bed. It was just right right. She fell asleep. Then the bears came home.

They noticed their porridge had been eaten. They saw the tiny broken chair. Then they went into their bedroom.

They saw their beds ruffled. Then they saw Goldilocks sleeping in Baby Bear's bed.

Goldilocks woke up and saw the bears. She jumped out the window and ran home. **The End.**

GA1144

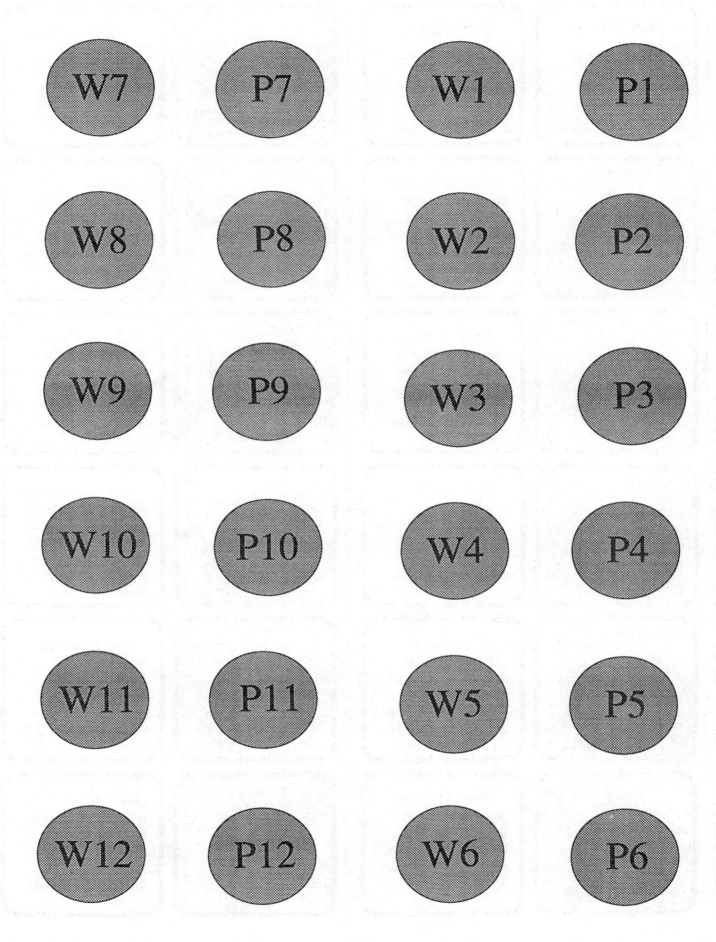

38

GA1144

The Three Little Pigs

*Illustrated by
Pat Harroll*

© 1990 by Good Apple

The Three Little Pigs

*Rewritten by
Flora Joy*

© 1990 by Good Apple

Once upon a time there were three little pigs. Their mother sent them out to seek their fortune.

The first little pig met a man with a bundle of straw. He asked the man to give it to him and he did.

The first little pig built himself a house of straw. He moved in and was quite happy in his new home.

The second little pig met a man with a large bundle of sticks. The man gave the sticks to the pig.

Then the second little pig built himself a house from those sticks. He too lived quite happily.

The third little pig met a man with a wagon full of bricks. The man gave the bricks to the pig.

Then the third little pig built a house from those bricks. Soon he began living a fun and easy life.

After all three houses were built, the big bad wolf knocked on the door of the first little pig's house.

"Little Pig, Little Pig, let me come in," cried the big, bad wolf. "Not by the hair of my chinny-chin-chin," said the first pig.

"Then I'll huff and I'll puff and I'll blow your house in!" cried the wolf. And that's what he did!

The first little pig was scared! He ran to the house of his older brother, the second little pig.

GA1144

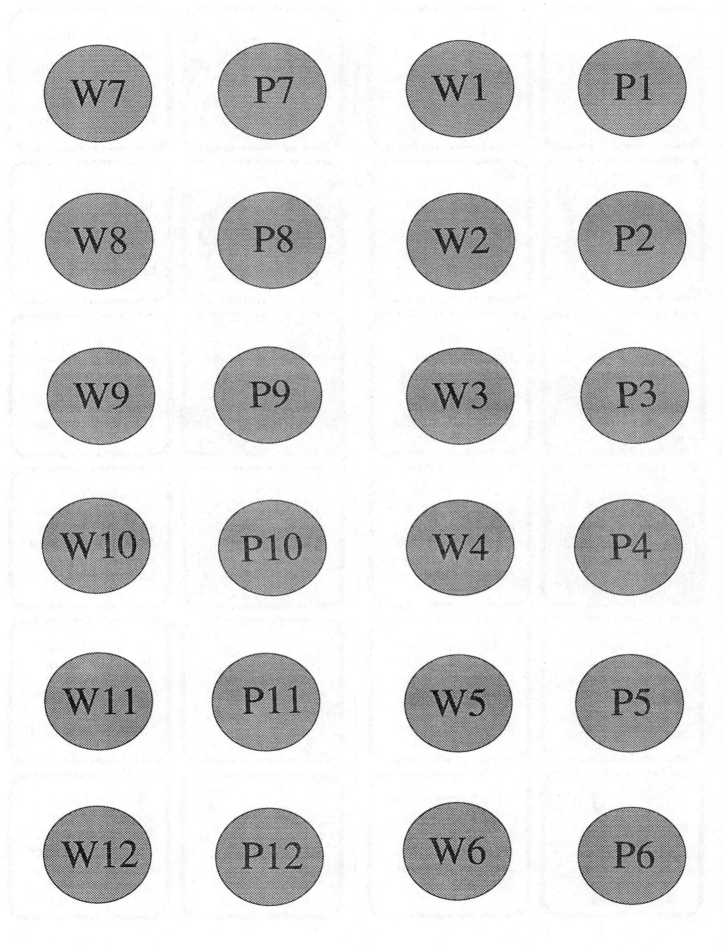

Soon after he was inside the house of sticks with his brother, there was a loud knock on the door.

"Little Pigs, Little Pigs, let me come in," cried the wolf. "Not by the hair of our chinny-chin-chin," both yelled.

"Then I'll huff and I'll puff and I'll blow your house in!" cried the wolf. And he blew down the house of sticks.

Both little pigs squealed from fear. They ran to their older brother's house of bricks.

Soon after they arrived, they heard the big bad wolf knocking loudly on their door.

"Little Pigs, Little Pigs, let me come in," he cried. "Not by the hair of our chinny-chin-chin," all three sang.

"Then I'll huff and I'll puff and I'll blow your house in!" cried the wolf as he took a big breath.

And he huffed and he puffed and he puffed and he huffed. But he just couldn't blow it down!

Then the wolf saw the chimney. He decided to crawl up on the roof and go down the chimney.

But the little pigs heard him. They put a pot of boiling water at the bottom of the chimney.

Down the chimney came the wolf into the pot of boiling water which the pigs had ready for him.

Then the three little pigs sang, "Who's afraid of the big, bad wolf?"

THE END

41

GA1144

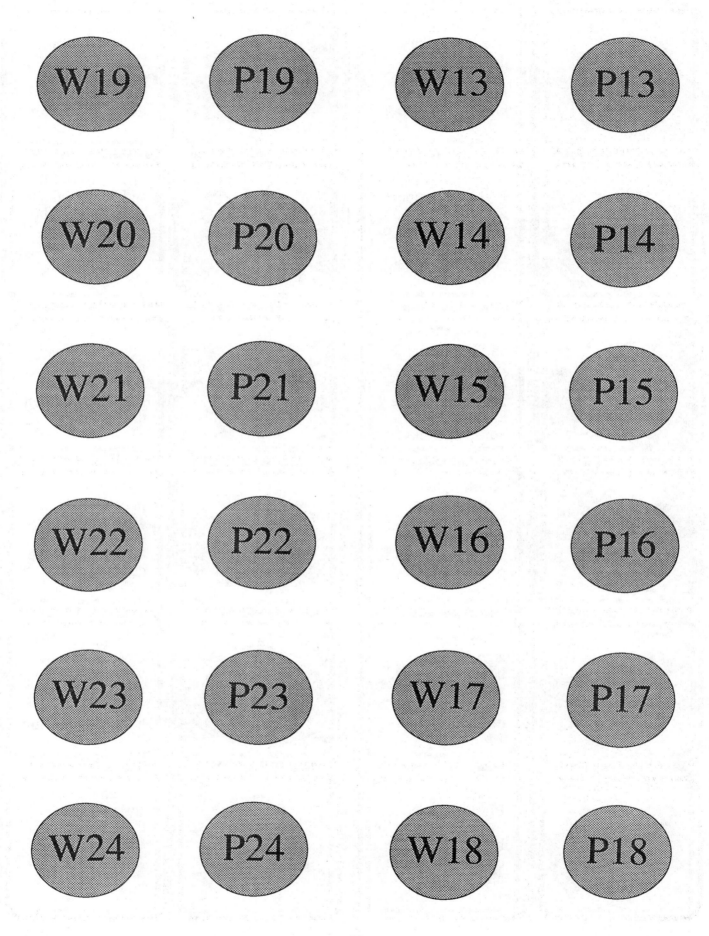

42

43

GA1144

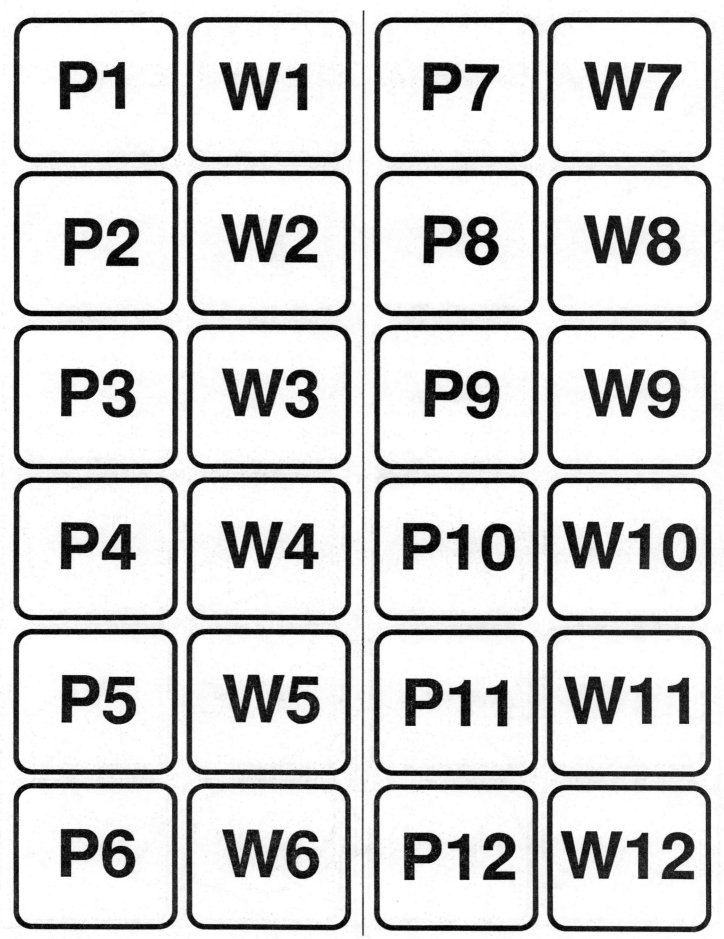

44

SEQUENCE SECTION D: PASSAGE MANIPULATIVES

This section builds on the previously explained skills in Sections A-C, but it involves only word groups (lines, sentences, or paragraphs) without pictures as clues in determining the appropriate sequencing.

Pages 47-56 provide examples which may be used in this manner. All designs, strips, or frames are positioned in their correct order. These pages may be prepared as described in the first part of Section B.

Pages 47, 49, and 51 contain eight sentences which sequentially explain the steps in the preparation of the indicated design. Pages 53 and 55 provide samples of word groups without an associated design. Some are brief sentences or paragraphs each placed in a separate frame to be positioned in order. Some involve the typing of a complete passage and cutting the **lines** of the typed passage into separate rearrangeable strips. In this last style, both semantic and mechanical clues aid in the arrangement of the strips. Several additional sets of this style may be easily prepared by teachers or students. For example, a paragraph summary of a reading selection may be typed (triple-spaced) and cut into strips for students to arrange in a sequential order. Newspaper articles (of interest to the readers) may be prepared for students to arrange in paragraph order. (Please consider the same cautions as explained for cartoon strips in Section B.)

The provided items in Sections B-D may all be housed in small envelopes or library card pockets. An inexpensive method is to buy boxes of white 3 1/2" by 6 1/2" mailing envelopes. Seal each one and cut in half. For a box which will house all of these prepared envelopes, see the back side of this page.

Preparing Boxes for Comprehension Cards

The two box patterns shown below may be prepared to house the cards provided in this text. The larger pattern will house the sequence cards housed in small (halved) mailing envelopes. The smaller pattern will house the Character Trait cards provided on pages 85-87 and the Real or Unreal cards on page 94. To prepare boxes, cut the shapes from heavy paper (preferably 6-ply poster paper) at the outside solid lines. Crease with a razor blade at the dotted lines. Fold into a box shape. Tape at edges. Wrap decorative self-adhesive paper completely around the box shape, trimming away the excess decorative paper. Trim with edging tape, if desired.

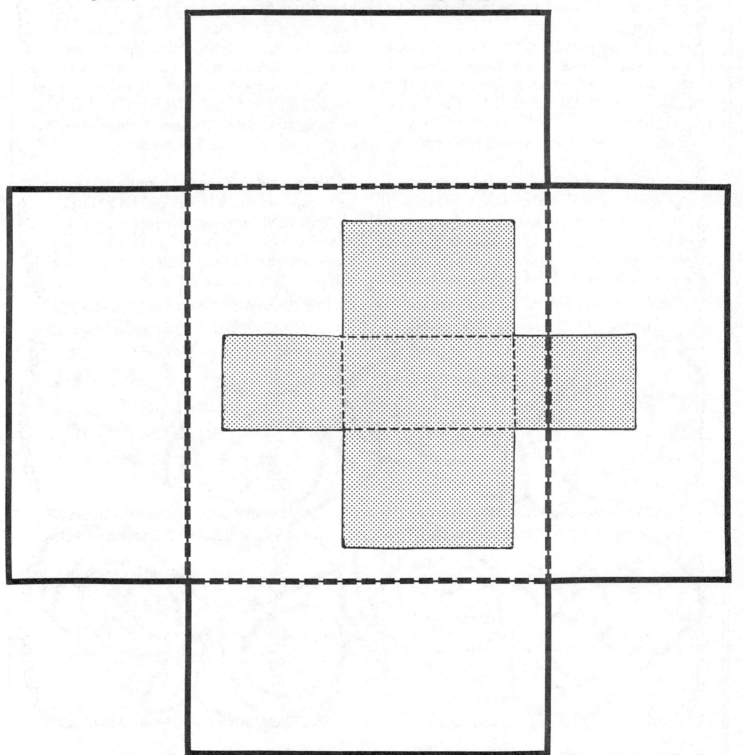

GA1144

How Chalk Is Made

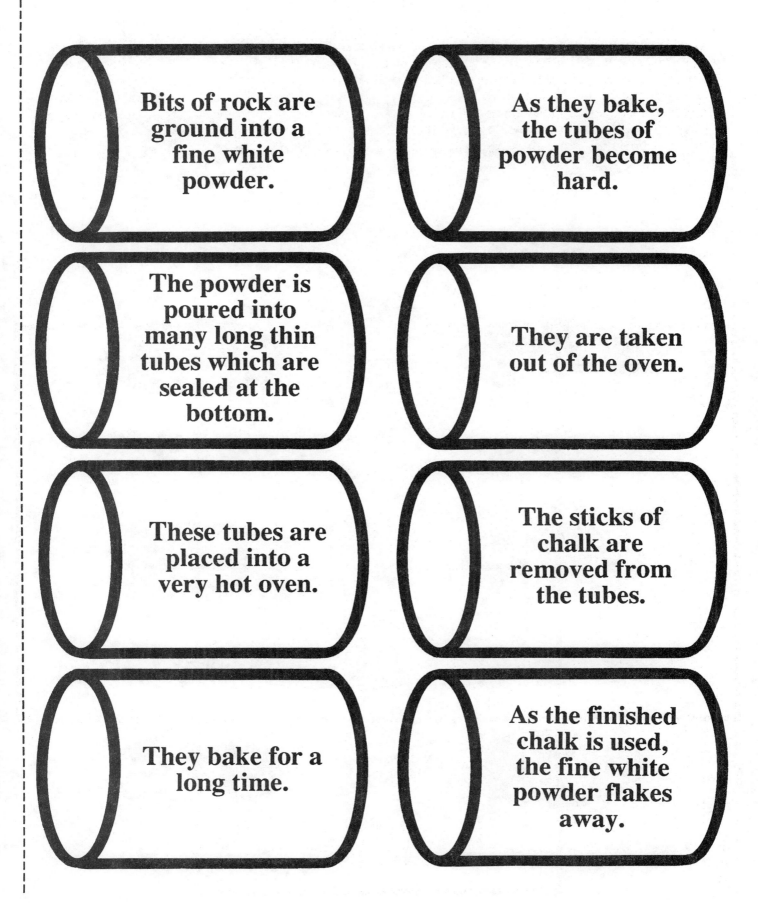

Bits of rock are ground into a fine white powder.

As they bake, the tubes of powder become hard.

The powder is poured into many long thin tubes which are sealed at the bottom.

They are taken out of the oven.

These tubes are placed into a very hot oven.

The sticks of chalk are removed from the tubes.

They bake for a long time.

As the finished chalk is used, the fine white powder flakes away.

GA1144

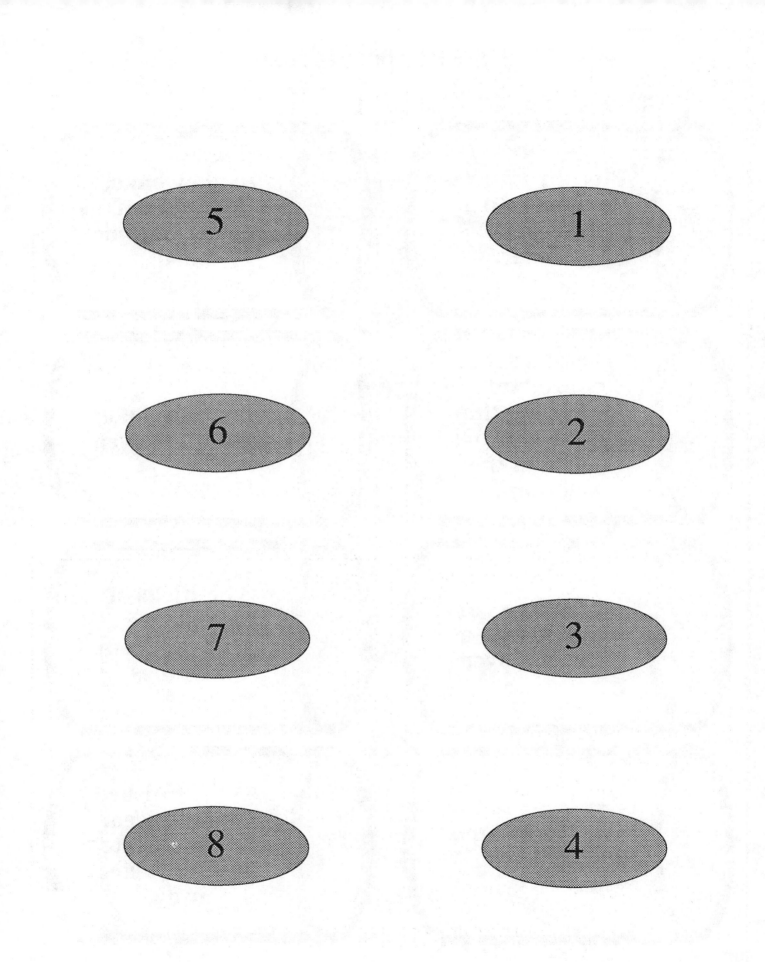

48

How Crayons Are Made

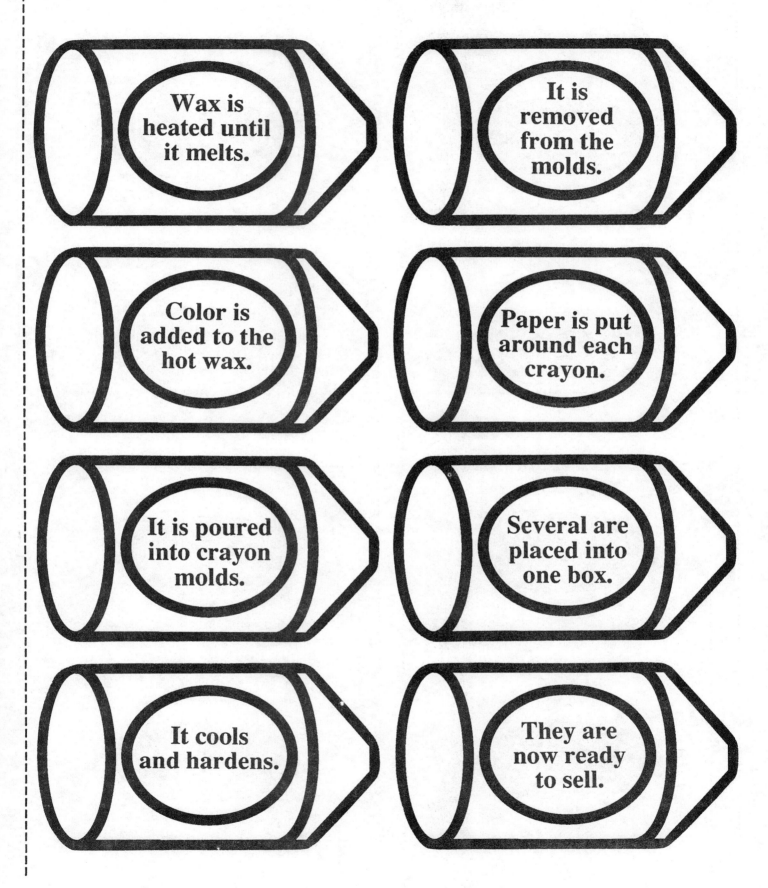

Wax is heated until it melts.

It is removed from the molds.

Color is added to the hot wax.

Paper is put around each crayon.

It is poured into crayon molds.

Several are placed into one box.

It cools and hardens.

They are now ready to sell.

49

GA1144

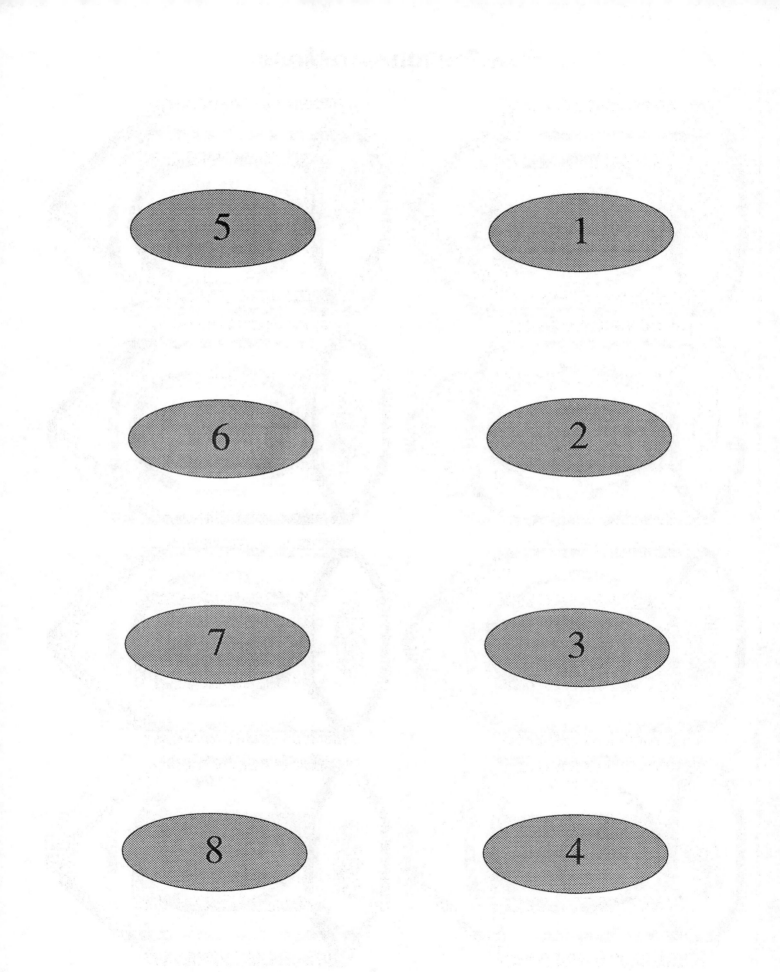

50

How Pencils Are Made

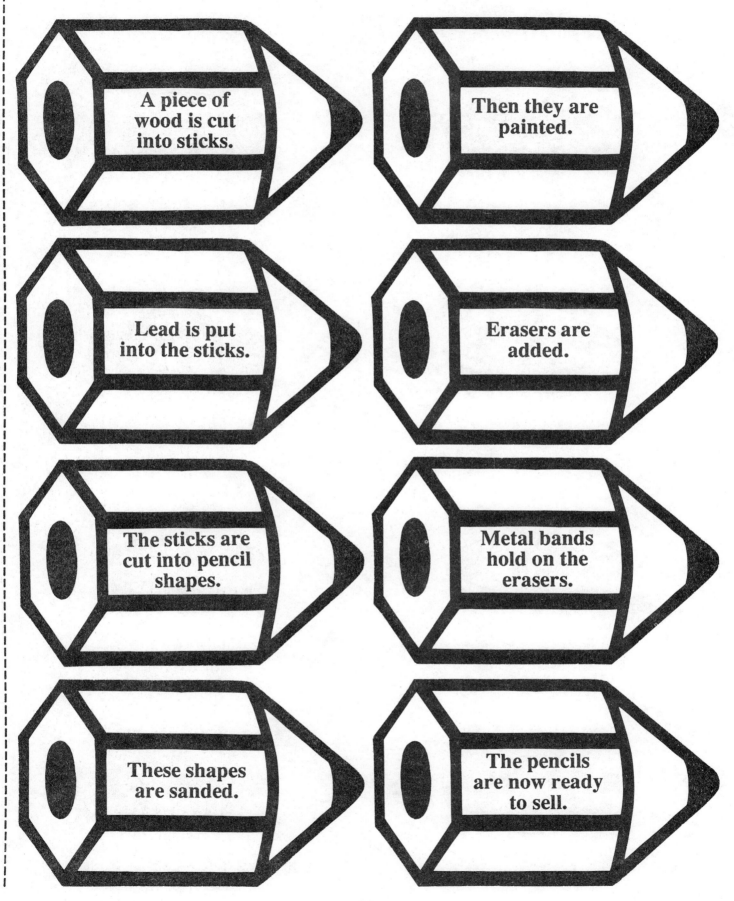

A piece of wood is cut into sticks.

Then they are painted.

Lead is put into the sticks.

Erasers are added.

The sticks are cut into pencil shapes.

Metal bands hold on the erasers.

These shapes are sanded.

The pencils are now ready to sell.

51

GA1144

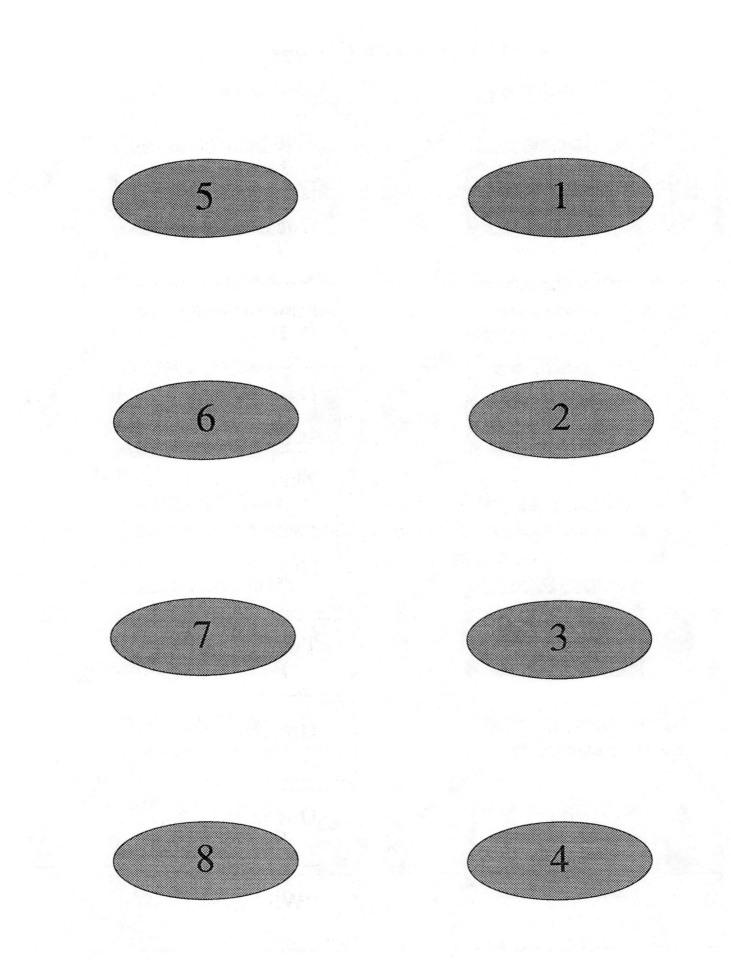

GA1144

Ten Little Leaves

by Flora Joy

Ten little leaves
   Hanging on a vine

One fell off
   That left nine.

Nine little leaves
   Hanging on a gate

One fell off
   That left eight.

Eight little leaves
   Floating toward Heaven

One didn't make it
   That left seven.

Seven little leaves
   Fell in the sticks

One blew away
   That left six.

Six little leaves
   Looking alive

One fell over
   That left five.

Five little leaves
   Fell by the door

One blew away
   That left four.

Four little leaves
   Hanging on a tree

One fell off
   That left three.

Three little leaves
   Away they flew

One got tired
   That left two.

Two little leaves
   Having some fun

One fell asleep
   That left one.

One little leaf
   Said with a groan,

"Why did everyone
   'Leaf' me alone?"

 GA1144

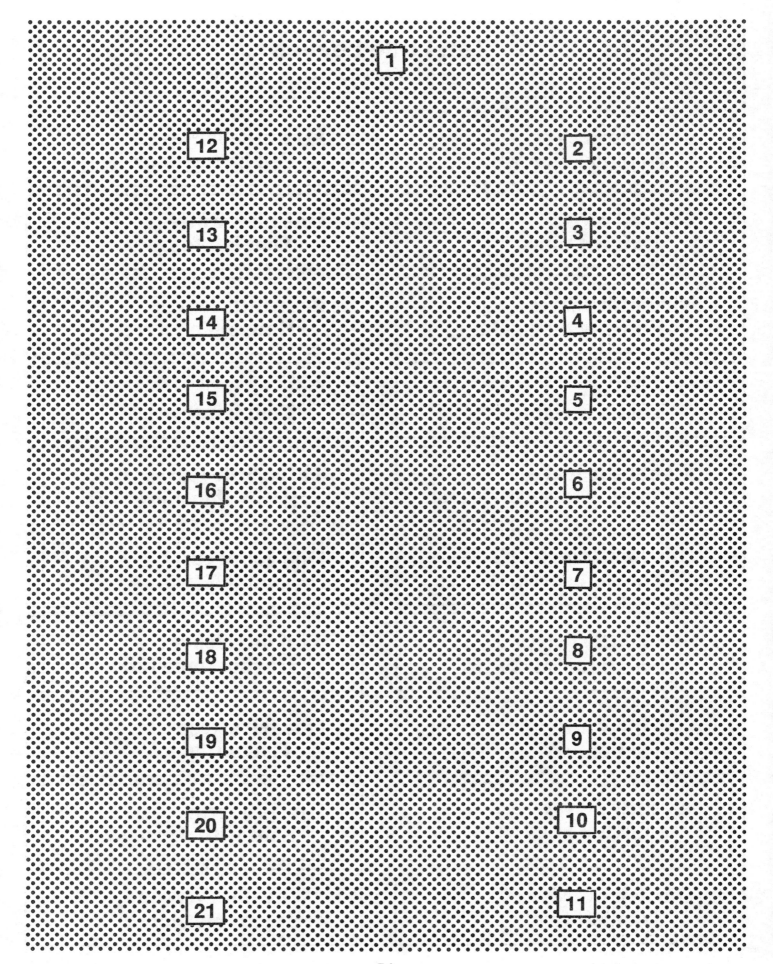

GA1144

The Lost Rabbit

by Flora Joy

Once upon a time a little rabbit ran away from home. Soon he was lost in the forest.

He hopped first to one place then to another, trying to find his way back home. Soon he met a hungry fox.

"Can you help me find my way home?" the little rabbit asked the fox.

"Come closer. I can't hear you," answered the fox.

But the little rabbit was afraid to walk closer to the fox. So he hopped on through the forest. Soon he met a hungry snake.

"Can you help me find my way home?" the rabbit asked the snake.

"Come closer. I can't hear you," answered the snake.

But the little rabbit was afraid to walk closer to the snake. So he hopped on through the forest. Soon he met a hungry wolf.

"Can you help me find my way home?" the rabbit asked the wolf.

"Come closer. I can't hear you," answered the wolf.

But the little rabbit was afraid to walk closer to the wolf. By now it was dark. The little rabbit had hopped for quite a long time. He had wandered first in one direction and then in another. He was tired. He was hungry. He wanted to find his way home.

Just then he heard the sound of another animal. He was afraid. He hid in the bushes. The little rabbit heard the animal say something.

"Oh, where could he be?" The voice was familiar. It was the little rabbit's mother!

Little rabbit jumped out from the bushes. He was so happy to see his mother. She showed him the way home.

After that the little rabbit decided not to run away from home ever again!

GA1144

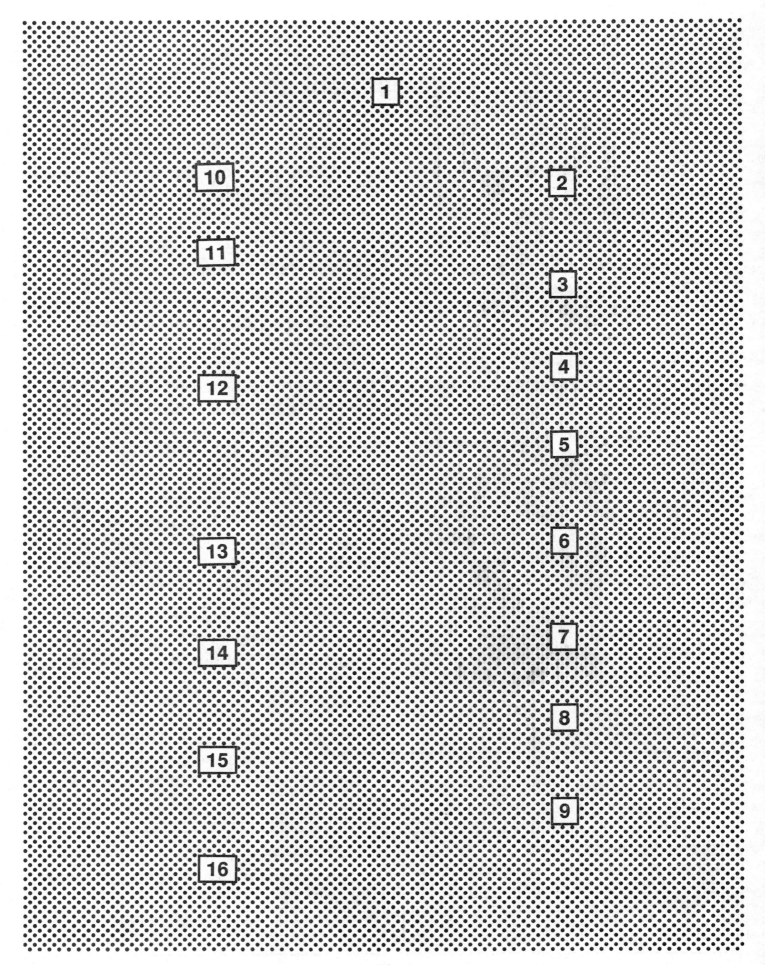

56

SEQUENCE SECTION E: WRITTEN QUESTIONS

In addition to manipulatives, a variety of written questions may be prepared to build the comprehension skill of sequence. A sequence question may be simply worded to require a true/false, a multiple-choice, or a completion answer from the reader. Consider the following examples with some thoughts involving the question construction and use.

SHORT-ANSWER SEQUENCE QUESTIONS

Below are some typical and conventional short-answer sequence questions.

> *The next thing the fox did after he chased the rabbit was _____.*

Caution: Sometimes this type of question can penalize the clever and competent thinker. Consider the answer "breathed a sigh of relief" which **could** have actually happened **before** the next stated event in the passage.

> *Circle the word which best fits the sentence: (Before, While, After) the boy was lost in the forest, he screamed and screamed.*

Note: It is assumed that this question is based upon the comprehension of a portion of a selected passage. This, therefore, forces the reader to examine the **order** of the events. Caution: If the question already denotes **one** and **only one** logical response—*with or without a written passage*, then the reader's answer might better reflect this general skill of logic rather than the comprehension of a specific passage. Sample: *"(Before, While, After) the boy was lost in the forest, he prayed that someone would come to rescue him."* What **other** answer could there possibly be, no matter if the passage has even been read? However, the latter sample **is** excellent for developing sequencing logic when **no specific passage** is being used.

WRITTEN NUMERICAL SEQUENCING

This style asks the reader to indicate the sequence of events in a passage by writing corresponding numbers beside a provided list of sentences in mixed order. Before using this as an on-paper activity for young learners, practice with several chalkboard examples to insure they are ready. If they are not, **please postpone** this section.

> *Below are six sentences. These sentences explain what happened in a story. They are in mixed order. The number 1 appears by the first thing which happened in this story. Write the number 2 by the one which happened next. Write the number 3 by the next one and continue until each sentence has a number.*
>
> _____ *He recognized the voice as one he had heard before.*
> ___(1)___ *Benny Bear heard a loud noise outside his window.*
> _____ *She had come by to invite Benny to come to a party at her house the next day.*
> _____ *As he walked over to see what it was, he heard a little girl's voice.*
> _____ *Benny decided that the party would be fun, so he told her he would be there.*
> _____ *It was Goldilocks, Benny's good friend from the past!*

GA1144

Reading selections for young children often have too many events for all to be included in the preceding style of question. Since it is crucial for these stated events to be logical and cohesive when they are read aloud in the correct order, this style may be modified slightly. There are three possibilities for this type of question for longer passages: **section sequencing, paragraph sequencing**, and **line sequencing**.

Section sequencing involves having the learners place in order the events which occur *in only one section of the story*. Paragraph sequencing involves rewriting the story *in brief paragraphs* and having the paragraphs (instead of single sentences) placed in order. (See "The Lost Rabbit" in Section D for an example.) Line sequencing involves paraphrasing the entire story and cutting into lines this triple-spaced typed summary for learners to arrange in order line at a time. This style may involve added mechanical factors such as paragraph indentation or punctuation as added clues to the appropriate sequence. Below are examples of section sequencing and line sequencing.

There was much action in this story. Between the time the lion discovered he had been tricked and the time the fox confessed his ugly prank, the lion talked with many animals. These animals are listed below in mixed order. The number 1 appears by the first animal the lion talked with. Write the number 2 by the one he talked with next. Write the number 3 by the next one and continue until each animal has a number. (In order to help with this question, part of the conversation is provided.)

_____*Bear ("No, I didn't hear a thing.")*
_____*Squirrel ("I heard you ask the beaver the same question.")*
___1___*Mouse ("Was that Mr. Fox?")*
_____*Beaver ("I can't answer that, but I'll bet Ms. Squirrel can.")*

The story about the tiger has been rewritten in much shorter form. It has been typed and cut into strips of single lines. These lines have been placed inside this envelope. Remove the strips and place them in the correct order. When you finish, remove the copy of the uncut story and compare your placement with this uncut copy.

A sample story for the envelope is given below. The story would be cut where the lines appear. These strips, along with an uncut copy, would be placed inside a mailing envelope.

The tiger felt he was the most important character in the entire forest. One day he met a small frog who wanted the tiger to bring him some food. The tiger, since he was so important, could not take the time to help the little frog. The little frog almost died before another animal brought him some food.

Much later the tiger walked to the river to get a drink. Then he fell into the river. He yelled for help. A frog was nearby. After thinking for a long while, the frog decided to help the tiger, even though the tiger had not helped him earlier when he was starving.

Because of the kind frog, that tiger then learned a valuable lesson.

CAUTIONS FOR WRITING SEQUENCE QUESTIONS

The following are some types of sequence question pitfalls to be avoided when possible. Each type of question is given a name in order to help point out the deficiency of such an example.

Caution 1: The Inappropriate Number

Who was the king's third son?

GA1144

This type of question is **generally** a simple detail, with no relationship to the *ORDER* of events. The fact that the word **third** is used does not always denote *sequence* (although it is *possible* to do so). Be careful!

Caution 2: The Cop-Out

> *List in order everything that happened in this story.*

This is the ultimate cop-out! Consider for a moment how **you** would like to answer such a question. Again, clever thinkers could be severely penalized with such a request. Sometimes in a relatively brief multi-sentence passage, dozens of "happenings" could have occurred, both stated and implied. A better version (though still not very exciting) is "List (in order) the **four** things that happened to the elephant in this story."

Caution 3: The Overload

The following question uses this text portion: "*. . .The cat chased the mouse behind the barn, through the garden, into the orchard, back to the house, beneath Mr. Smith's car, and onto the highway. The mouse thought he was safe as he crawled into the small pipe by the road. . . .*"

> *Trace the mouse's steps by writing the number 1 by his first spot, number 2 by his second, etc.*
> _____*Highway*
> _____*Barn*
> _____*Mr. Smith's car*
> _____*Pipe*
> _____*Garden*
> _____*House*
> _____*Orchard*

Consider the above question. Besides being so poorly worded, **who cares?** These facts were included in the reading passage to aid in building reader suspense, not because the move from one position to another had any bearing on the future outcome of the story. They do not matter as far as the order of events is concerned.

Before using this type of question, consider this thought: *Was the order of this list **important** enough to have all students consider which one happened **before** another, etc.?* The wording of this style of question is in the same category as the question, *"What is the third word in the second paragraph?"* Again, **who cares?** Do not use valuable class time with such nonsense!

Another thought: If such a question has **several** items to arrange in order, consider what happens when the reader gets one (and only one) item out of order. If that occurs near the beginning, all following answers may be inappropriate, even though **only one** error has been made. How should such an answer be scored? Please remember also that the visual arrangement of such a list can cause confusion for many young learners.

Caution 4: The Giveaway

Sometimes the wording of the sentences to be placed in order can be an automatic "giveaway" regarding the sequence of events. Consider the following sentences (which are intentionally placed in order) for such a question.

> *Place these sentences in order:*
> _____*It all started late one night. . . .*
> _____*Mr. Tellies was beginning to. . . .*
> _____*He. . . .*
> _____*Finally he. . . .*

Enough giveaway clues are present to arrange these sentences in order **even without** the remainder of the words. (In some cases, however, such helpful clues are desired.)

Caution 5: The Lift-Out

The following sample is the opposite of the above. In this case sentences are lifted from the actual text of the story. However, such wording can cause a high level of confusion.

> *Place these sentences in order:*
> _____*Snow White's stepmother was jealous.*
> _____*Snow White's stepmother had a magic mirror.*
> _____*The woodsman was a kindhearted man.*
> _____*The seven dwarfs had a small cottage in the forest.*

NONE of the above choices have **anything** to do with the **order** or events in the reading passage. All were sentences which *appeared in the text* in a particular place, but in no case did they relate to an **order**. For example, "Snow White's stepmother was jealous." She was a jealous woman **throughout the entire story,** not just at the moment this fact was mentioned in print. The same applies to the mirror, the woodsman, and the dwarfs. **Be very careful** with lifting sentences from the text.

Caution 6: Thought Omissions

This is perhaps the trickiest problem in the preparation of a sequence question. After selecting some thoughts for learners to place in order, MAKE SURE that these **make sense when they are read aloud in order.** The following question has *omitted thoughts* between **every** step, therefore making it impossible for learners to determine unity in the task. (Try it!)

> *Place these sentences in order:*
> _____ *"Who's the fairest of us all?"*
> _____*But the woodsman did not have the heart to kill Snow White.*
> _____*She saw seven little beds.*
> _____*She handed her the apple.*
> _____*The prince was stricken by her beauty.*
> _____*She fell down dead from rage.*

In addition to the vast confusion caused from independently extracting various thoughts from this story, consider confusion created by the pronoun **she** and its different referents.

After selecting the sentences to be used in this type of question, **always read them aloud in the right order** to determine if the thoughts are continuous and coherent. They **must** make good sense when read in succession before learners should answer such questions.

Caution 7: Poor Student Instructions

Notice that the above three examples all have the instructions, "Place these sentences in order." This frequently leaves young learners confused regarding specifically what they should do to answer the question. Do they cut up the page? Do they use numbers? Do they use letters? Wording should be complete and thorough. (See an example of well-worded instructions under the heading "Written Numerical Sequencing.")

SOME HELPFUL HINTS

The writing of sequence questions **appears** easy to those who have not engaged in such practice. However, much thought should be given to such a task. The following are some helpful hints.

Hint 1. Carefully examine the question stem or instructions. Wording such as "Put these in order" can cause much confusion regarding how the task should be completed. For sentences to be placed in order, **always** place the number 1 by the **first one** in the sequence.

Hint 2. Always paraphrase sentences to be placed in order. **Never** lift them from the text.

Hint 3. Always make sure the items to be placed in order are **important ones.**

Hint 4. Do not use the present tense for the wording of the items to be placed in order. For example, *"The little girl runs and hides"* should be *"The little girl ran and hid."* The events in the story have *already happened* .

Hint 5. Make sure each question can fit onto one page. Do not continue onto another page.

GA1144

TEACHING THE COMPREHENSION SUBSKILL OF DETERMINING THE

 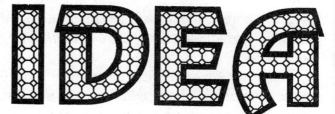

MAIN IDEA

The skill of determining the main idea of a story or passage involves having the reader or listener identify the central thought or the author's intended message in the story. Sometimes this idea is directly stated in a passage, sometimes it is only implied, and sometimes it is written at the end as a "moral." More often than not, however, the reader or listener will need to glean through the printed (or spoken) words to determine just what the central message was.

Determining the main idea is neither easy for the teacher to teach nor for the learner to master. Often when young readers are requested to state the main idea of a passage they have just read or heard, they quickly *summarize* the selection instead of considering the underlying message. Stress on "facts only" has led students into attending to the *who, what, when,* or *where* in a selection. Therefore, the teacher of such skills may need to consider creative and pictorial methods, especially with younger students.

Five different styles are provided in this document to support the creative teaching of main idea skills. These styles offer a wide grade range of use. They begin with those intended for the very beginning reader and continue to those designed for the more mature learner.

SECTION A: MATCHING TITLES WITH PICTURES

The skill of determining the main idea is a relatively difficult one for nonreaders and non-writers to master while using on-paper activities. Students at this stage of development are greatly aided when a *visual* association can be made. One such method for nonwriters is to match a *picture idea* with a title. Since titles require *reading* skills, these needed skills may be basic and minimum. For example, if only **one** easy word (such as **pig**) could be recognized, then an appropriate match can be made. Pages 66-67 provide such examples. On these pages only these basic words need to be read to make appropriate associations: **bull, pig, whale** or **ship, zoo** or **giraffe, cat, girl** or **snake, ants** or **cap,** and **bird** or **car.**

Simple directions are printed on these sheets. More complete directions are: *"Look at the pictures on the page. There are four pictures and four titles. Write the picture number by the title which it matches."*

The above may be used with students possessing very basic reading skills. For students slightly more mature in reading proficiency, pages 68-69 may be used. These pages offer four different pictures on the same central object. Therefore, the learner must more closely attend to both the picture and the words in the titles. On page 68, for example, the word **dog** is used in three of the four titles. A dog is shown in all four pictures. On page 69, the word **lion** is in all four titles and a lion is shown in all four pictures.

It should be noted that there is a very close association with identification of basic sight words and the completion of this task. As indicated in the introductory material of this document, many reading tasks have intentional overlapping skills.

For **very early** learners, an instructor may show this page to an individual or small group. The students may be given time to examine the pictures before the instructor reads aloud the titles. The matching and all discussion may be done orally.

This section may also be photocopied for immediate use as consumable pages. For a permanent **manipulatable** activity, laminate the photocopied pages or cover them with clear self-adhesive paper. Cut out the four pictures and the four titles. Have the learners independently match the pictures with their corresponding titles. Numerical answers may be written on the backs of the titles to cause the activity to be self-checking. The pictures may be colored, if desired.

SECTION B: SELECTING MAIN IDEA PICTURES

A slightly more difficult step than that offered in Section A is to have learners select a **picture** which expresses the main thought of a passage they have just read or heard. Pages 70-73 are examples of this style. Only one of the four pictures presented *accurately* relects the main thought of the passage. The remaining distractors, however, contain thoughts *relating* to the selection—they just do not reflect the **main** thought.

These pages may be photocopied and used as consumable materials or they may be prepared in a permanent fashion. See Section A for details.

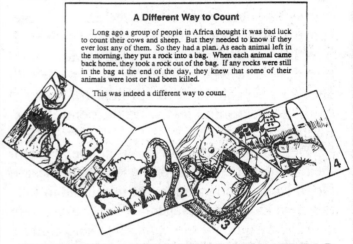

A Different Way to Count

Long ago a group of people in Africa thought it was bad luck to count their cows and sheep. But they needed to know if they ever lost any of them. So they had a plan. As each animal left in the morning, they put a rock into a bag. When each animal came back home, they took a rock out of the bag. If any rocks were still in the bag at the end of the day, they knew that some of their animals were lost or had been killed.

This was indeed a different way to count.

SECTION C: SELECTING MAIN IDEAS FROM PROVIDED PHRASES

This section is perhaps the most common style of question for selecting the main idea. Learners hear or read a passage. They select one of several provided phrases (or clauses) which best states the main thought of the passage. Pages 74-75 provide examples of this style.

The Anteater

The anteater gets its food in a different way from other animals. It has a very long and sticky tongue. It drags its tongue through insects which are on the ground. The insects stick to the tongue. The anteater then pulls its tongue back into its mouth and eats the insects.

Think about the main thought in the above story. Read the following five choices. Which one best states this main thought? Write your answer on separate paper.

_____ A. The problems of insects
_____ B. How an ant eats
_____ C. Sticky things
_____ D. How an anteater gets food
_____ E. Insect meals

GA1144

SECTION D: THE "BANNER" STYLE FOR MAIN IDEA

A creative method for enticing learners to determine the main idea is to request the words which they might choose to write on a "banner" (or other similar visual). Careful coaching will be needed during the students' initial efforts. Pages 76-80 provide thirteen different examples which may be used in this fashion. The following are some sample introductory wordings for selected provided visuals.

"Newspaper headlines provide the main thought of the reported event. If the 'XXXX' story were to have a headline in tomorrow's newspaper, what words should be used? (Remember that the headline should reflect the main thought of the story!)"

"Mr. Jones has just written the story 'XXXX' and wants people to know what it is about. He has built a wooden sign to wear as he walks up and down the street. On his sign he wants words which will tell the central message of his story. Write a sentence which could tell people this idea."

"Bill Board wants all third-grade students to read the story 'XXXX.' In case they cannot find a copy, he wants them to know the main thought of the selection. Write a sentence which he should use for this advertisement."

"Because of Seth's bad manners, Rover has decided to leave home. He packed up all of his belongings in a truck and left during the middle of the night. He is angry about what has happened to him. He wants everyone else to know about this, so he decided to write a warning on his truck. However, since he is a dog, he cannot write. Please write this message for him."

This last example refers to a specific story in which the "warning" is actually the main idea in the story. Each story has many clever and distinctly different ways of enticing the learners to think through and state the central message. Many additional shapes or visuals may be drawn, depending upon the content of the reading passages.

SECTION E: THE WRITTEN QUESTION

Because of the difficulty of preparing visuals, many instructors resort to the use of written questions for teaching main idea. Before writing such questions, please do the following:

- Ask yourself, "Does this selection even **have** a main idea?" Not all reading passages or stories do have. Some are simply expository or descriptive materials. Most basal readers using a word patterning style (*"Can Nan fan Dan? Run, Spot, run. Run, run, run!"*) for text will not have a main idea in their selections. **Skip this skill** for these types of materials.

- If the passage **does** have a main idea, **YOU write it down.** If you have great difficulty in so doing, please be aware of the fact that young learners will have *even more difficulty.*

- After writing the main idea of the selection, ask yourself, "Was this thought **OF SIGNIFICANCE**?" Or does this revelation elicit a "Who cares?" reaction?

- **If** the main idea **is** of significance, then decide what type of question will help the learners to put this thought into their own words or to select it from several provided choices. The following are some possibilities.

Creative Main Idea Questions

Each reading passage has its own unique possibilities for the designing of main idea questions. The following are some starters.

*You have just read "Mouse Magic." You want to tell your cousin in California about this story. You are now dialing his number. Because of the telephone costs, you may talk for only **ten seconds.** You want to be sure to include the main message in this story. What will you say?*

GA1144

"Mystery at the Cove" has three adventures. Something can be learned and remembered from each one of these three adventures. A three-act play could be written for each of these sections. Tell what might be the lesson learned in each of these three acts.

Act 1:

Act 2:

Act 3:

The above story has a very valuable lesson. You want to share this lesson with a former classmate who has moved to Canada. Send him (her) a telegram which tells this lesson. You may use up to twenty words.

Consider supplying telegram forms for the above style of question.

". . . Mike's favorite rock group is coming to Ellisville! Mike set his alarm for six o'clock. He and his dad got up and went to the ticket office. Mike stood in a long line for several hours. Finally he bought his ticket. As he returned to the parking lot, he met Jerry. Jerry also came to buy a ticket. But by the time Jerry reached the front of the line, all of the tickets had been sold. . ."

The lesson to be learned in the above story could be written as a proverb. Which of the following proverbs best states this lesson?

____ A. Birds of a feather flock together.

____ B. The early bird gets the worm.

____ C. A bird in hand is worth two in the bush.

____ D. Don't count your chickens before they hatch..

Although the understanding of proverbs is a fairly difficult task for young learners, they do provide much material for thoughtful discussions.

The Traditional Main Idea Question

The comprehension subskill of determining the main idea is a frequently measured skill in national reading tests for all ages, even college students and adults. The traditional question has five or six parts with each part playing a specific function. Below is an example of such a question.

Which of the following best expresses the main thought of this story? (This is called the question stem.)

____ A. (One answer is only a detail of the reading selection. This indicates whether the reader can distinguish between the main idea and a fact within the passage.)

____ B. (One answer is too general to be selected as the main idea. This indicates whether the reader can distinguish between the main idea and the global topic for the whole selection.)

____ C. (One answer is correct.)

____ D. (One answer does not relate at all. This can indicate whether or not learners are thinking, if they understand what is meant by main idea, or if they are just guessing.)

____ E. (One answer is just a terrific distractor.)

By asking learners the above style of main idea question, the instructor can eventually determine the type of teaching which needs to be planned for this specific skill. For example, if many students respond with a choice which is actually only a detail, then instruction should center around the distinction between the main message and a detail of the passage.

GA1144

The wording of the above question stem can be greatly varied. The following is an example: *"Sidney Fletcher had an idea he wanted to share when he wrote 'The Adventures of Tom Finn.' Which of the following **best** expresses this idea?"*

Whatever wording is selected, it should fit the passage. Also note that the **order** of the right answer and the distractors should be altered with each question. ("C" should not always be the right answer.)

CAUTIONS FOR WRITING MAIN IDEA QUESTIONS

Although there are many clever and creative ways to entice learners to reflect on the main thought of a reading selection, caution should be taken with various types of questions. Consider the following thoughts.

> *What is the main idea of this story?*

This is the epitome of cop-outs! It reflects no creativity, no cleverness, and no **interest** on the part of most learners! Use it only when you have had the flu for three months and do not have the energy to think!

> *Choose the best title for this story.*
> ___ A. *My Worst Moment*
> ___ B. *Why I Should Mind My Mother*
> ___ C. *A Strange Man on Mars*

What constitutes the **best** title? In **whose opinion** is it the best? The author's? The reader's? The instructor's? Is the *best* title the one which is the most creative, the most *far-out,* or the one which actually states the main thought? If this wording is used, please communicate that the title selected **should** reflect the main idea. Many readers would be attracted to the answer *"A Strange Man on Mars"* even if it doesn't relate. It (in their opinion) is the **best** title to help brighten up a dull passage.

Final thought: When writing any main idea question, always remember that the main idea is **not** the summary of the selection. Think of the main idea as the underlying message of the passage. If we could remember only one thing from a story, what might it be?

65

MATCHING TITLES WITH PICTURES—SET 1

(Write the number of the picture by the title which it matches.)

Bull stops traffic___   ___Whale upsets ship

Pig is family pet___   ___Zoo now has giraffes

66

MATCHING TITLES WITH PICTURES—SET 2

(Write the number of the picture by the title which it matches.)

Cat needs owner____   ____Ants cover boy's cap

Girl has pet snake____   ____Bird found in car

GA1144

MATCHING TITLES WITH PICTURES—SET 3

(Write the number of the picture by the title which it matches.)

Dog saves girl's life____   ____Dog guards animal

Dog is for sale____   ____Poodle wins contest

GA1144

MATCHING TITLES WITH PICTURES—SET 4

(Write the number of the picture by the title which it matches.)

Lion attacks calf____   ____Lion found on road

Lion has six cubs____   ____Lion seen in yard

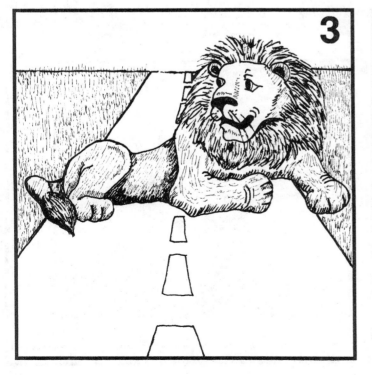

69

GA1144

An Elephant Herd

A group of elephants is called a herd. A herd may have only ten elephants in it. Or it may have as many as fifty. Each herd has a leader. This leader is often a mother elephant. Most of the others in the herd are younger elephants.

The herd is much like a family. They travel together. They eat together. They protect each other from danger. They all work together as a team.

Read to the student: The above story has a main idea which is shown in one of the four pictures below. Look carefully at each picture and decide which one it is.

GA1144

A Different Way to Count

Long ago a group of people in Africa thought it was bad luck to count their cows and sheep. But they needed to know if they ever lost any of them. So they had a plan. As each animal left in the morning, they put a rock into a bag. When each animal came back home, they took a rock out of the bag. If any rocks were still in the bag at the end of the day, they knew that some of their animals were lost or had been killed.

This was indeed a different way to count.

Read to the student: The above story has a main idea which is shown in one of the four pictures below. Look carefully at each picture and decide which one it is.

GA1144

The Scary Monster

A few years ago Matt thought a large monster lived at his house. The monster scared Matt at night. It lived in Matt's closet. After the lights were turned off, it would make terrible noises.

When Matt tried to sleep, the monster would come out of the closet. It would walk toward Matt's bed. Matt was frightened. He shook with fear.

Later Matt learned the truth. He had only *thought* there was a monster in his closet. There had never been a monster at all. Just thinking about one, however, had always scared Matt. It was almost as bad as if one had really been there!

Read to the student: The above story has a main idea which is shown in one of the four pictures below. Look carefully at each picture and decide which one it is.

GA1144

Cats

Some cats spend their lives as pets. They often live inside people's homes. Many are given toys to play with, food to eat, and warm beds to sleep in. Their days are spent indoors. They live in a safe but dull place. These cats are called house cats.

Other cats do not live in a house. They live outdoors. Many stay in dark and dirty alleys. They are often in much danger. Many are hurt or killed because they are not safe. But there is much adventure. These cats are called alley cats.

Cats need both comfort and adventure. The house cat sees little adventure. The alley cat sees little comfort.

Read to the student: The above story has a main idea which is shown in one of the four pictures below. Look carefully at each picture and decide which one it is.

GA1144

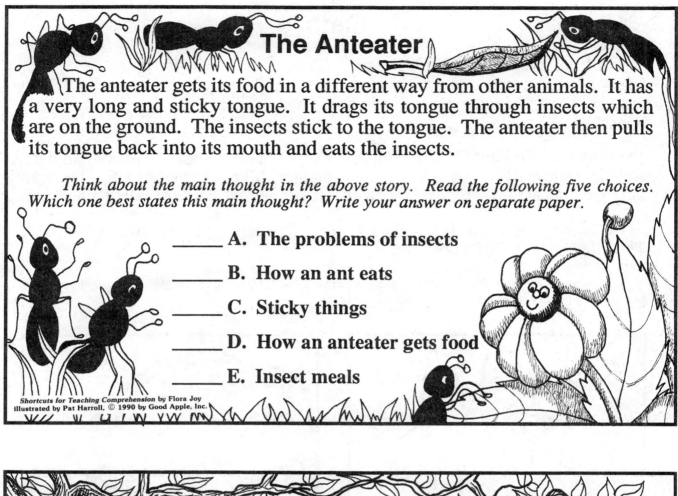

The Anteater

The anteater gets its food in a different way from other animals. It has a very long and sticky tongue. It drags its tongue through insects which are on the ground. The insects stick to the tongue. The anteater then pulls its tongue back into its mouth and eats the insects.

Think about the main thought in the above story. Read the following five choices. Which one best states this main thought? Write your answer on separate paper.

_____ A. The problems of insects

_____ B. How an ant eats

_____ C. Sticky things

_____ D. How an anteater gets food

_____ E. Insect meals

Shortcuts for Teaching Comprehension by Flora Joy
illustrated by Pat Harroll, © 1990 by Good Apple, Inc.

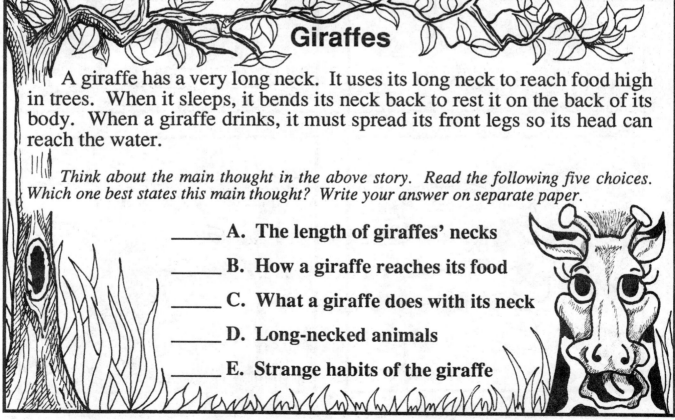

Giraffes

A giraffe has a very long neck. It uses its long neck to reach food high in trees. When it sleeps, it bends its neck back to rest it on the back of its body. When a giraffe drinks, it must spread its front legs so its head can reach the water.

Think about the main thought in the above story. Read the following five choices. Which one best states this main thought? Write your answer on separate paper.

_____ A. The length of giraffes' necks

_____ B. How a giraffe reaches its food

_____ C. What a giraffe does with its neck

_____ D. Long-necked animals

_____ E. Strange habits of the giraffe

GA1144

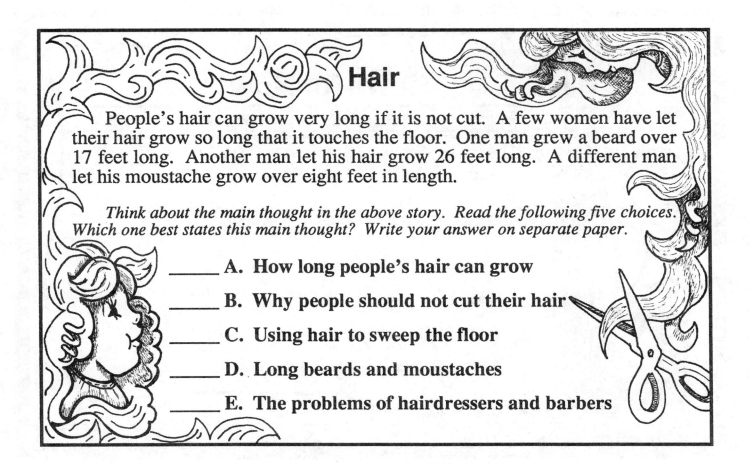

Hair

People's hair can grow very long if it is not cut. A few women have let their hair grow so long that it touches the floor. One man grew a beard over 17 feet long. Another man let his hair grow 26 feet long. A different man let his moustache grow over eight feet in length.

Think about the main thought in the above story. Read the following five choices. Which one best states this main thought? Write your answer on separate paper.

_____ **A. How long people's hair can grow**

_____ **B. Why people should not cut their hair**

_____ **C. Using hair to sweep the floor**

_____ **D. Long beards and moustaches**

_____ **E. The problems of hairdressers and barbers**

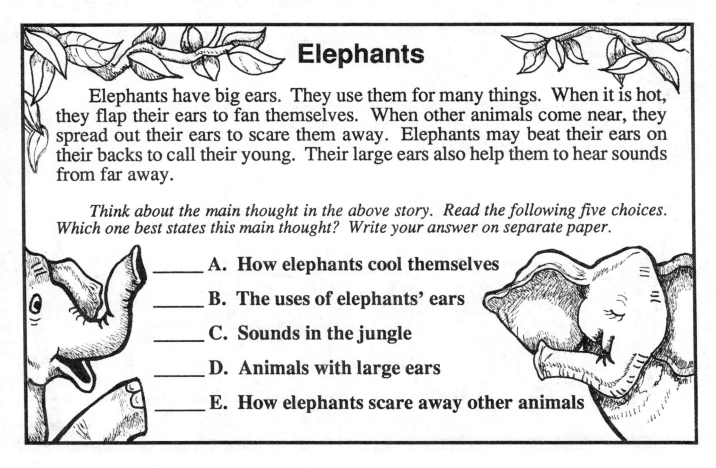

Elephants

Elephants have big ears. They use them for many things. When it is hot, they flap their ears to fan themselves. When other animals come near, they spread out their ears to scare them away. Elephants may beat their ears on their backs to call their young. Their large ears also help them to hear sounds from far away.

Think about the main thought in the above story. Read the following five choices. Which one best states this main thought? Write your answer on separate paper.

_____ **A. How elephants cool themselves**

_____ **B. The uses of elephants' ears**

_____ **C. Sounds in the jungle**

_____ **D. Animals with large ears**

_____ **E. How elephants scare away other animals**

GA1144

News for Now!

Vol. 102 . . . . . 35 cents daily . . . . . $1.00 Sunday . . . March 4

EXTRA! EXTRA!

GA1144

GA1144

Shortcuts for Teaching Comprehension by Flora Joy
Illustrated by Pat Hartoll. © 1990 by Good Apple, Inc.

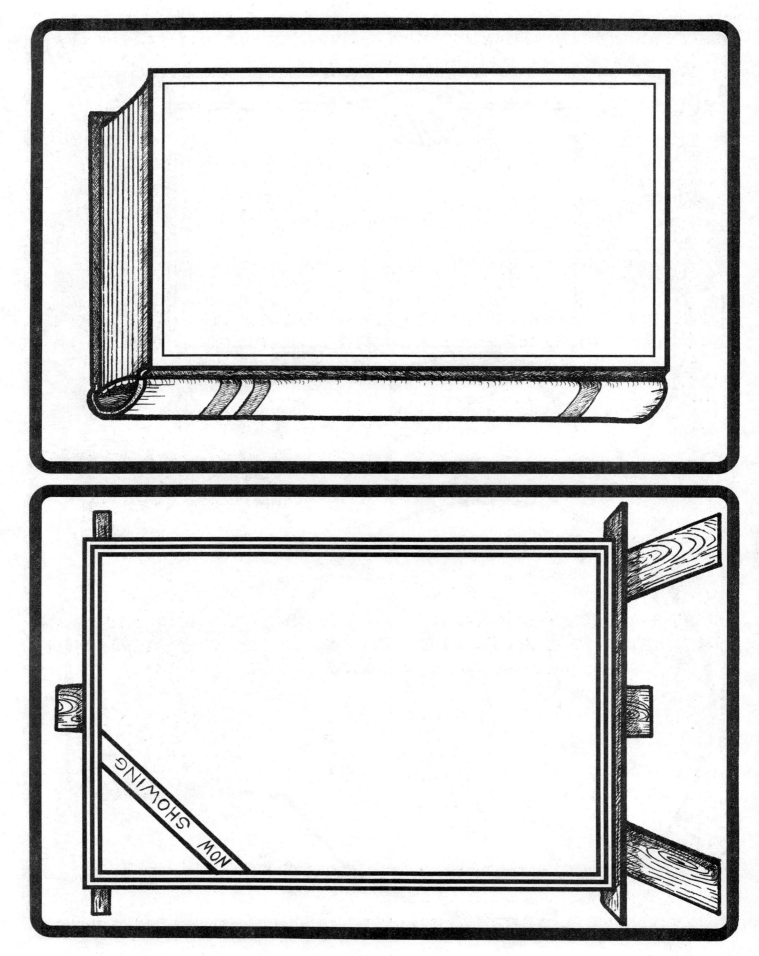

GA1144

79

GA1144

80

GA1144

TEACHING
THE COMPREHENSION SUBSKILL OF DETERMINING
CHARACTER
TRAITS OR
PERSONALITY DESCRIPTIONS

The comprehension subskill of determining character traits (or personality descriptions) involves having the reader or listener select a trait which fits a specific character described in a passage. A variety of different types of questions may be prepared for this purpose. Below are some examples.

SECTION A: CHARACTER PICTURE AND WORD CARDS

Sixteen male characters and sixteen female characters are shown on pages 85-86. Each drawn character reveals one specific trait. As an introductory exercise, these picture cards may be shown to an individual or group who will attempt to determine which trait is shown. This is a forerunner for the learning of the vocabulary terms associated with these traits. (It would be impossible for a learner to match a character with the word *cowardly* without knowing the word.)

Although the pictures on these two pages could match more than one of the words shown on pages 88-90, the following words are considered appropriate choices: *angry, bashful, boastful, bossy, brutal, charming, contrary, crabby, dishonest, famous, good, happy, jealous, mannerly, sad,* and *wicked.*

Some traits are frequently associated with animals. Common expressions and sayings prevail regarding these associated traits. Examples are *wise as an owl* or *eager beaver.* Although animals do not necessarily have "character traits," this skill may be learned through the use of animals. Page 87 shows sixteen pictures of animals. These may be discussed by the learners. Again several matches may be made with the word cards shown on pages 88-90. The following are some suggestions: *bold, bossy, brave, cowardly, cross, eager, gentle, graceful, greedy, grumpy, naughty, proud, sly, strong, weak,* and *wise.*

The remainder of the word cards may be used as desired. Additional character traits may be used when desired. (See Section D.)

There are many other uses for these pictures and cards. One example is to give each learner a word card and have him or her act out the trait. The remainder of the class will try to guess what the trait is. (This may also be done **without** the use of the cards.)

Another example is to place all the picture cards (with the pictures showing) on a table. A character from a recent story is named. Learners select the picture which could be most closely associated with the named character.

GA1144

Allow learners to discover other games and activities with these cards.

SECTION B:
THE WRITTEN QUESTION

Several types of written questions may be prepared for this skill. These questions may appear in the traditional formats or they may be unique and different. Below are some starters.

> *Could Jane be described as being* **childish** *in this story? Why or why not?*

Note that the question style *Could _____ be described as being _____ in this story?* can be used with practically any character and any character trait in any story. This is an especially good type of question for oral discussions. **Always** follow this question with *Why or why not?* This forces the learner to explain his or her choice of answers rather than responding with an arguable *yes* or *no*.

> *Which character in this story was the most* **impolite?** *Why?*

This is another style of question which may be repeated with almost any reading selection: *Which character in this story was the most _____?* The character traits selected should be in the speaking vocabularies of the learners.

> *Mr. Lee was a very unusual person. Name a television star or movie star who is much like him. (The character of this person may be like the character shown on the screen rather than the private character.)*

The above question may be prepared with multiple-choice answers, if desired.

> *Which member of your family is most like* **Clyde** *in this story? Why?*

Be careful with this one! This question and its "cousin" above have many variations. Another student in the room, a neighbor, a politician, someone in the school, etc., may be used instead of family member or film star.

> *Which of the following words best describes Pat at the first of the story before she started to school?* **fair, fussy, crabby, cool**

> *For many reasons Sue changed in this story. Write the letter "F" by the word which best describes how she was at the* **first** *of the story. Write the letter "L" by the word which best describes how she was at the* **end.**
>
> | | |
> |---|---|
> | *kind* | *mannerly* |
> | *tricky* | *thoughtful* |
> | *warm* | *strange* |

SECTION C: OTHER
CHARACTER TRAIT ACTIVITIES

Several additional activities may be enjoyed for developing the skill of determining character traits. Below are some suggestions.

For classes of learners who can read the words for character traits, list from ten to twenty character traits on the chalkboard. Whisper one of the twenty words to one student and have him or her enact the trait. The remainder of the learners try to select the enacted trait from those listed on the chalkboard. After the trait has been guessed, it is erased. A new student is selected and another trait is whispered.

A caution is offered for all of the above types of questions. At times it is difficult for young learners to separate a character trait from a physical trait. The word *ugly,* for example, may be used as either. Much discussion could occur regarding this concept.

See the "Reader Reaction" for correlated activities with character traits.

GA1144

SECTION D: ADDITIONAL CHARACTER TRAITS

Although the majority of the character traits listed below are too difficult for primary students, the list is still offered—just in case! Either ignore them or have fun with them!

abrupt, abusive, accommodating, acquiescing, active, adept, adroit, adventuresome, affable, affectionate, agreeable, aggressive, agonizing, alert, alive, alluring, aloof, altruistic, ambiguous, ambitious, ambivalent, amiable, amicable, amnesic, amorous, anarchical, angelic, animalistic, animated, antagonistic, apathetic, apologetic, appreciative, apprehensive, arbitrary, argumentative, aristocratic, arrogant, artistic, ashamed, asocial, assertive, astute, attentive, auspicious, austere, authoritative, autocratic, aware, awed, awkward, backward, barbaric, barbarous, battered, befuddled, begrudging, beholden, belligerent, benevolent, bewildered, bewitching, biased, big-headed, bigoted, bitter, bizarre, blameless, bland, blank, blasé, bleak, blissful, blithe, bloodthirsty, blue, blunt, boisterous, boorish, boring, bothersome, brainless, brainy, brash, brazen, bright, bristling, brusque, burdened, businesslike, calloused, candid, cantankerous, capable, captivating, careful, care-free, casual, caustic, chagrined, chaotic, charitable, chaste, chatty, cheat, cheerless, cheery, childlike, chivalrous, civil, clean-cut, clear-cut, cloudy, coarse, cocksure, coersive, coherent, cold-blooded, collected, colorful, colorless, comforting, comical, communicative, compassionate, competent, competitive, complex, composed, compunctious, conceited, concerned, conditioned, confused, confident, congenial, conscientious, considerate, consistent, constrained, constructive, contemplative, contemptible, contemptuous, contented, contradictory, controversial, convivial, cool-headed, cooperative, cordial, corrupt, courtly, covetous, coy, crafty, crass, crazed, creative, credible, critical, crooked, crude, crusty, cunning, curbed, curious, curt, cutting, dainty, daredevil, daring, dashing, dazed, debased, deceitful, decent, deceptive, decisive, defeated, defenseless, defensive, difficult, defiant, deft, degraded, degrading, dejected, delirious, deleterious, delicate, delighted, delightful, delinquent, demanding, demeaned, democratic, demonical, demure, dense, dependent, depressed, depressing, deranged, derelict, derogatory, desolate, desperate, despicable, despondent, destitute, destructive, detectable, determined, devil-may-care, devious, devoted, dextrous, dictatorial, dignified, dimsighted, diplomatic, disagreeable, disastrous, discerning, disciplined, disconsolate, discontented, discourteous, discreet, disgraceful, disgruntled, disgusting, disheveled, dishonorable, disillusioned, disloyal, dismal, disobedient, disorderly, disorganized, disrespectful, dissatisfied, distant, distasteful, distinguished, distinctive, distraught, disturbed, divine, docile, dogged, domestic, domineering, doomed, doubtful, dour, downcast, downhearted, dramatic, dreadful, dreamy, dreary, dubious, dull, dutiful, dynamic, easy-going, eccentric, ecstatic, effervescent, efficient, egotistical, elated, elegant, eloquent, elusive, embarrassed, embittered, eminent, emotional, enchanting, endearing, enigmatic, enjoyable, enraptured, enrapturing, enraged, enslaved, enterprising, enthused, enthusiastic, entranced, enviable, envious, erudite, established, evasive, exacting, exceptional, excitable, explosive, expressionless, expressive, extreme, extroversive, extroverted, extroverting, exultant, facetious, faithful, faithless, fallible, fanatical, farcical, farsighted, fascinating, fastidious, fatherly, fault-finding, faultless, favorable, fearless, fearful, fearing, feeble, fervid, fickle, fiery, firm, fit, flaming, flexible, flighty, flippant, foaming, forbearing, forcible, forgetful, forgivable, forgiving, forlorn, formal, forthright, fortunate, foul, foxy, frank, frantic, fraternal, fraught, free, frenzied, fresh, frugal, frustrated, fulfilled, funny, fuming, furious, galant, generous, genial, genuine, giddy, glad, gleeful, gloomy, gluttonous, good-natured, graceless, gracious, grateful, gratified, green, grim, groovy, gross, gruff, guiltless, guilty, guillible, happy-go-lucky, hard-shell, harebrained, harmful, harmless, harum-scarum, hasty, haughty, headstrong, heart-rending, heavy-hearted, heavy-laden, heedless, helpful, heroic, high-and-mighty, high-handed, high-hatted, high-principled, high-strung, hilarious, homely, homicidal, honorable, hopeful, hopeless, hospitable, hot-blooded, hot-tempered, huffy, humane, humble, humbled, humdrum, humiliated, humorous, hushed, hypercritical, hypocritical, hysterical, idealistic, idiosyncratic, idiotic, idle, ignorant, ill-behaved, ill-bred, ill-mannered, ill-tempered, illustrious, immature, immodest, immoral, impatient, impartial, impelling, imperceptive, imperfect, impersonal, impertinent, impetuous, important, impractical, impressive, imprisoned, impudent, impulsive, inattentive, incapable, incapacitated, incoherent, incompetent, inconsiderate, inconsistent, incorrigible, incredible, indelible, independent, indifferent, indignant, indiscreet, indiscriminate, indulgent, industrious, inefficient, infallible, infamous, infantile, inflammable, inflexible, influential, informal, infuriated, ingenious, inglorious, inhibited, inhibiting, iniquitous, injurious, innocent, inoffensive, inquisitive, insane, insecure, insensitive, insignificant, insincere, insolent, inspirational, instinctive, insubordinate, insulting, interesting, interrogating, intimidating, introversive, introverted, introverting, intuitive, inventive, invigorated, invigorating, irate, irksome, iron-handed, irrational, irrepressible, irreproachable, irresponsible, irreverent, irritable, irritating, jesting, joking, jovial, joyful, joyous, jubilant, judgmental, just, juvenescent, juvenile, keen, kind-hearted, lackadaisical, ladylike, larcenous, large-hearted, laudable, lawabiding, lawless, lax, leisurely, lenient, lethargic, level-headed, liberated, lifeless, light-hearted, likable, limp, listless, lively, loathsome, lovable, loving, lucky, mad, magisterial, magnetic, malevolent, malicious, manageable, maternal, matter-of-fact, mature, mealy-mouthed, meddlesome, meek, melancholy, melodramatic, menacing, mercenary, merciful, merry, methodical, meticulous, mild, militant, mindful, miraculous, mirthful, mischievous, miserly, modest, moody, moonstruck, monotonous, moral, morale-building, moronic, morose, mortified, motherly, moved, muddled, mule-headed, mulish, mutinous, myopic, mysterious, naive, negative, neglectful, negligent, neighborly, nervous, neutral, new-fashioned, noble, nonchalant, nonindulgent, nonpartisan, notorious, nutty, oafish, obedient, objective, obliged, oblivious, obnoxious, observant, obstinate, offensive, off-guard, old-fashioned, on-guard, open-hearted, optimistic, orderly, ordinary, organized, outgoing, outlandish, outraged, outrageous, overbearing, overconfident, overpowering, oversensitive, overtaxed, overwhelming, overwrought, painful, parasitic, partial, passionate, passive, paternal, patient, patronizing, peculiar, peevish, pensive, perceptive, perfect, perplexed, perplexing, persecuted, persistent, pert, perturbed, perverted, pessimistic, petty, philosophical, phovic, picayunish, pig-headed, pious, placid, pleasant, pleasing, poised, polished, polite, pompous, positive, possessed, possessive, practical, prejudiced, prejudicial, preoccupied, presumptuous, pretentious, private, procrastinating, productive, proficient, progressive, prosperous, protected, provincial, provocative, prudent, prodish, prying, psychotic, pungent, punitory, pure, puritanical, pushy, puzzling, qualified, quarrelsome, questionable, quiescent, racy, radiant, rash, rampant, rational, ravenous, raving, ready, realistic, reasonable, reckless, refined, refreshing, regretful, rejected, rejoicing, relaxed, reluctant, remorseful, repugnant, repulsive, reputable, resentful, reserved, resigned, resistant, resourceful, respectable, respected, respectful, respecting, responsible, responsive, revengeful, reverent, revolutionary, rewarded, right, righteous, rigid, rigorous, riotous, risky, romantic, rotten, ruffled, ruthless, sane, sarcastic, satisfactory, satisfied, saucy, savage, scandalous, scatheless, scatter-brained, scientific, scornful, scrupulous, seasoned, secure, sedate, seething, self-assured, self-centered, self-confident, self-conscious, self-controlled, self-depriving, self-disciplined, selfish, self-loving, self-reliant, self-righteous, self-sacrificing, senile, sensational, senseless, sensible, sensitive, sensual, sensuous, sentimental, serene, servile, settled, sexy, shadowy, shaky, shallow, shamed, shameful, shameless, sharing, sharp, sheltered, shiftless, shocking, showy, shrewd, significant, simple, sincere, sinful, skillful, slanderous, slavish, slick, sluggish, smooth, smug, snappy, snarling, sneaky, snobbish, snug, sober, sociable, softened, solemn, solitary, somber, soothed, sound, special, spectacular, spineless, spirited, spiritless, spiritual, spiteful, spotless, square, squeamish, stable, stagnant, stainless, stern, stilted, stingy, stormy, straightforward, strait-laced, striking, stubborn, stuck-up, studious, subdued, sublime, submissive, subservient, subtle, successful, suggestive, suicidal, sulky, sullen, sunny, superb, supersensitive, sure-footed, surly, suspicious, sweet-tempered, swell-headed, sycophantic, sympathetic, systematic, tactful, tactless, talented, tame, tart, taxed, taxing, tedious, telepathic, tempermental, tempestuous, tenacious, tender, tender-hearted, terrorized, terrorizing, thankful, thick-headed, thin-skinned, thorny, thorough, thoughtless, threatening, thrifty, thrilled, thunderstruck, timid, tipsy, tolerant, touched, touching, touchy, trained, traitorous, tranquil, triumphant, troublesome, trusting, trustworthy, truthful, trying, turbulent, two-faced, tyrannical, unaccommodating, unambitious, unappreciative, unashamed, unassuming, unbecoming, unbending, unbiased, unblemished, uncertain, unchangeable, uncivil, uncommunicative, uncompromising, unconcerned, unconquerable, uncontrollable, uncooperative, uncouth, understanding, undesirous, undiscerning, undisciplined, uneasy, unembarrassed, unemotional, unenthused, unenthusiastic, unerring, unestablished, unexcitable, unexciting, unexpressive, unfair, unfaithful, unfaltering, unfavorable, unfit, unforgivable, unfortunate, unfulfilled, ungentlemanly, ungrateful, unhappy, unimaginative, unimpressed, unimpressive, uninquisitive, uninteresting, unique, unkind, unladylike, unlovable, unloved, unloving, unlucky, unmanageable, unmannerly, unmindful, unmoved, unnerved, unobservant, unoffending, unparalleled, unperturbed, unpleasant, unpolished, unprejudiced, unpretentious, unprincipled, unproductive, unqualified, unrealistic, unreasonable, unrefined, unresponsive, unrestrained, unruffled, unruly, unscrupulous, unseasoned, unstable, unsteady, unsuspecting, untainted, unthoughtful, untroubled, unwanted, unworthy, unyielding, upright, uprighteous, uproarious, vain, vainglorious, valiant, venturesome, veracious, verbal, verbose, vicious, victimized, vigilant, vile, villainous, vindictive, violent, virile, virtuous, vivacious, vivid, volcanic, voluntary, vulgar, vulnerable, wanted, warlike, warm-hearted, wary, wasteful, watchful, weak-minded, weary, weather-beaten, well-bred, well-meaning, white-livered, wholesome, willing, wily, winning, withdrawn, witty, woebegone, worried, wretched, zany, zealous, zesty!

GA1144

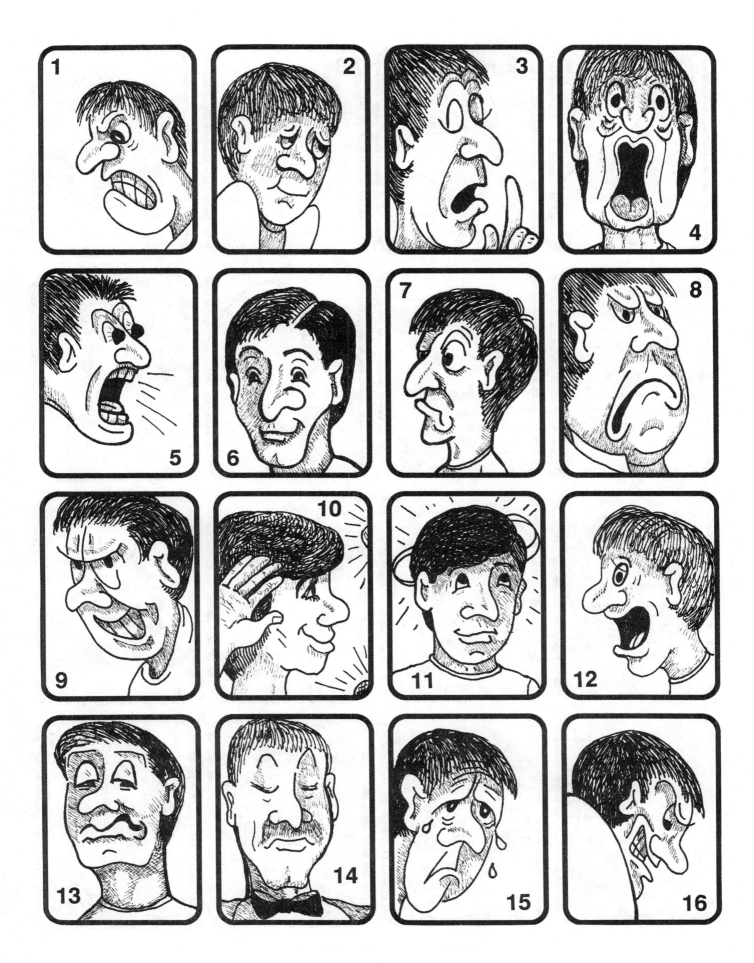

GA1144

87

angry	brutal	contrary
bashful	calm	cool
beastly	careless	courageous
boastful	charming	courteous
bold	cheerful	cowardly
bossy	childish	crabby
brave	clever	cranky

88

GA1144

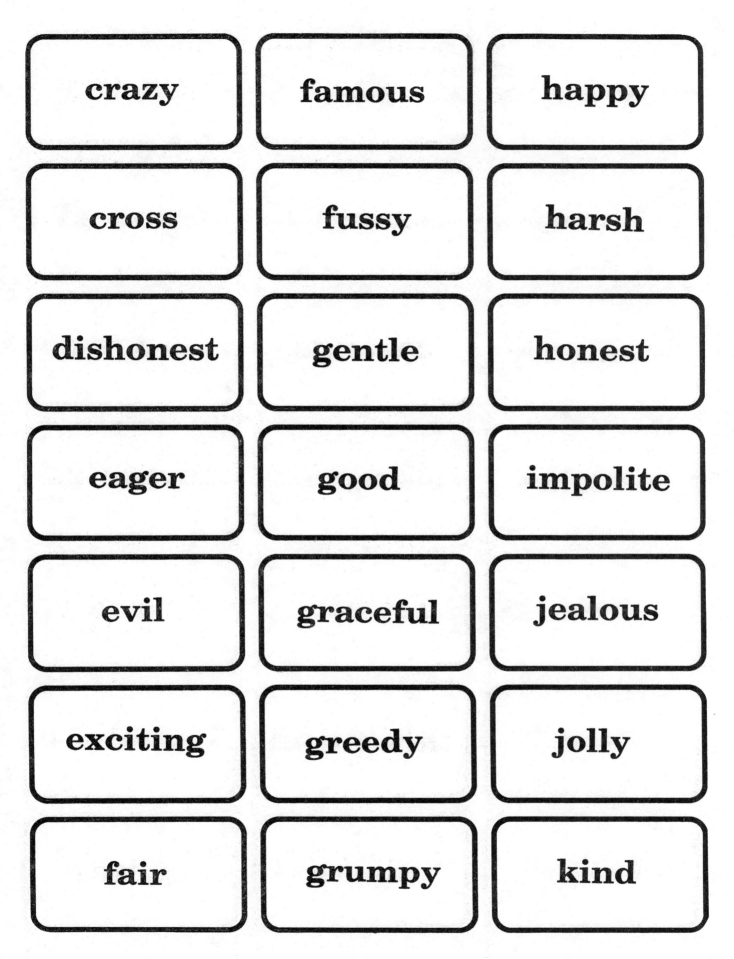

crazy	famous	happy
cross	fussy	harsh
dishonest	gentle	honest
eager	good	impolite
evil	graceful	jealous
exciting	greedy	jolly
fair	grumpy	kind

89

lonely	sly	tricky
loyal	smart	troubled
mannerly	strange	unselfish
naughty	strong	warm
proud	sweet	weak
sad	thoughtful	wicked
shy	tough	wise

GA1144

TEACHING
THE COMPREHENSION SUBSKILL OF
DETERMINING WHAT IS

REAL OR UNREAL

AND WHAT IS FACT OR OPINION

Much material written for young children involves friendly and animated characters. These characters, such as talking animals, are frequently presented as if they are real. All too often young learners are left quite confused.

Students also frequently confuse **facts** (which can be proven) with an **opinion** (which someone *thinks,* but which has *not* been proven). When a statement frequently appears **in print,** many soon believe it to be a **fact.** Students of all ages need experiences in making distinctions in these two categories.

Classroom activities may begin with younger children by reading aloud two different short passages—one which has happened and one which is make-believe. The class may discuss which one was real and **why.** At a later point students may examine science-fiction materials—not for the purposes of over-analysis, but for testing their abilities in making these determinations. It should be kept in mind that these stories should never be "ruined" by such discussions. These activities, however,

coupled with some suggestions below may aid in building this specific comprehension skill.

SECTION A: USING PICTURES

Page 94 contains sixteen different pictures of animals which are frequently encountered in children's stories. Some of these pictures actually resemble a **real** animal. Others are drawn in a manner which is not truly representative of that animal. Many are personified and many are given other characteristics not actually possessed by animals.

This page may be used as an intact sheet for discussion with young learners. It may also be prepared as separate cards to which learners may react independently.

As an extension of this provided page, pictures of animal characters in various stories may be located. Pictures of the same "real" animals may also be found. These may be compared. (Note that this activity also teaches the comprehension subskills of noting details and making comparisons or contrasts.)

GA1144

SECTION B:
THE WRITTEN QUESTION

A variety of written questions may be prepared for teaching this comprehension skill. Below are some examples.

After reading the story "The Very Hungry Caterpillar," write one factual sentence about how much caterpillars can eat and one fictional sentence about how much they can eat.

Factual Sentence:

Fictional Sentence:

"The Very Hungry Caterpillar" (by Eric Carle) is a delightful story about a caterpillar that eats many different things, including a lollipop, cherry pie, chocolate cake, and a nice green leaf. Through such a story students may give serious thought to what caterpillars do actually eat. This is not to suggest that all children's stories should be dissected and analyzed until the fun is gone. However, on occasion learners do need to discuss just what aspects of stories really are factual and which are included to help make an interesting story.

---

*"The Three Bears" is a fun story about a little girl and three bears. However, everything in this story could not actually happen in real life today. Write the letter **R** by the following statements which **could really happen** and the letter **N** by those which could **not really happen.***

_____ *1. Bears can walk through the forest.*
_____ *2. Bears eat porridge.*
_____ *3. Bears sleep in beds similar to those of people.*
_____ *4. Etc.*

---

*In the selection entitled "The Dangerous Elephant," the author presented some of **his feelings** as if they were **facts**. Some, however, were only his opinion. Read each of the following statements and tell whether they were the author's feelings or whether they are actually facts. Write the word **feelings** or the word **facts** by each one.*

_____ *1. The elephant is a powerful animal.*
_____ *2. The elephant was angry at Sally for not feeding him some peanuts.*
_____ *3. An elephant will remember you if you do something harmful to him, and he will get revenge later.*
_____ *4. The elephant's trunk can be used to lift very heavy objects.*
_____ *5. Etc.*

---

*Sometimes we hear statements repeated so often that we accept them as fact. Below are some thoughts for you to decide whether they are indeed true. Write the letter **F** by those items which are actual "provable" **facts**. Write the letter **O** by those statements which are likely only someone's **opinion**. Write the letter **D** if the statement **depends** upon other facts. Write the letter **N** by those statements for which there is **not enough information**.*

_____ *1. The Valley Forge Elementary School has the best basketball team in the nation.*
_____ *2. Sunbathing is harmful.*
_____ *3. Blondes have more fun.*
_____ *4. Henry Joy is the handsomest, sexiest human being on earth.*
_____ *5. All fat men are jolly.*
_____ *6. East Tennesseans talk funny.*

GA1144

After reading "Clyde's Collie," fill in the chart below with five facts and five opinions which are in this story. Use any source you would like to aid in determining your accuracy.

FACTS   OPINIONS

1.   1.

2.   2.

3.   3.

4.   4.

5.   5.

Note that the above question may be discussed orally instead of writing in a chart.

The writer of "The Lousy Law" has generalized about how fathers feel about family support. His conclusion was that fathers will **steal** in order to provide their family with food. Is this a true statement? Explain your answer.

Could the story "The Strange Parrot" happen **today**? Why or why not? Which parts **could** happen? Which parts could not? Explain your answer.

In the story "The Golden Wish," Lisa's arm turned into gold. Could this happen to you if you did as she did in this story? Explain your answer.

The following are some characters in the selection "Fools and Farces." Place a **Y** (yes) beside those character TYPES you are likely to meet in real life. Place an **N** (no) by those it would be impossible ever to meet in real life.

George   Monkey Roo   Bossy

Slossan   Jonah   Una

In the story "Karla's Closet," Karla had many dreams which she hoped would come true. Some of these dreams, however, cannot ever happen. List the five wishes she expressed and decide whether it is **possible** for each one of them to happen—or if they could occur only in the **fantasies** of her mind.

1.

2.

3.

4.

5.

You are a reporter for <u>The Inquiring Sun</u>. You have been sent to the scene of the story "The Fight at Dusk." Your assignment is to write a brief article about what actually happened **as you saw it**. **Remember:** Your paper can be sued if you print something which you **cannot prove!** Tell what you plan to write.

94

GA1144

TEACHING
THE COMPREHENSION SUBSKILL OF

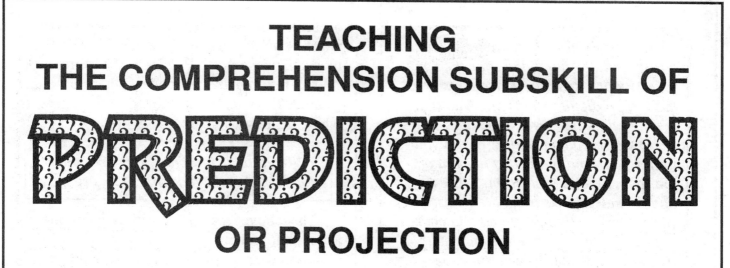

OR PROJECTION

This skill involves having the learner predict what the outcome might be at any point in the selection. The skill may be introduced by selecting a short fable which is likely unfamiliar to the students. Read the fable aloud except the last paragraph (or group of sentences). Allow discussion to ensue regarding possible endings.

In longer selections learners may project a different ending to the story or may predict how the outcome might have been different if a fact in the selection had been changed.

Unfinished stories (with a style such as "The Lady or the Tiger") are challenging materials to use in developing this skill. Minute Mysteries and Solve-A-Crime books may also be used.

Sometimes difficulty arises in giving a **numerical score** for the type of question that involves the reader's prediction choice. However, it is appropriate to give a "good" score for all *logical* responses by the learners.

SECTION A:
USING PICTURES AND CARTOONS

Page 97 contains nine pictures of scenes which have predictable outcomes. These pictures may be separated and distributed to individual learners who **draw or tell** what they think the outcome of the picture will/should be.

Cartoons clipped from the daily newspaper may be used to teach prediction or projection. Single or multiple frame cartoons may be used. Wordless or scripted cartoons may both be used, depending upon the reading abilities of the learners. The words may be removed from any printed cartoons, if desired. Page 98 contains four samples of cartoons which may be used for this purpose. Students may predict a response which could be written in the conversation bubble. This sheet may either be duplicated for the students to write on or it may be photocopied and mounted onto heavy paper for permanent use. In the latter case learners may either say their answers aloud or they may write them on separate paper.

SECTION B: USING REAL
LIFE EXPERIENCES

Experiences in real life may be used for prediction and projection. Activities or events at school, in the nation, or others reported in the newspapers may be used as the basis for the questions. The following are some examples.

> *Pretend that our class is planning to challenge Miss Smith's class in a game of soccer. Predict the winner.*

> *How might things be different in our nation now if the people had elected (select a name) for President instead of (the current President)?*

GA1144

> *In today's newspaper there is an account of all the candidates for the Jonesville Mayor. Read these accounts and make a prediction regarding who the winner might be. Write the name on a small strip of paper and sign with your initials. Drop it in the box in front of the room labeled "Election." The day after the election is over, the "classroom votes" will be counted and compared with the actual election results. (Other current news events may be treated accordingly.)*

Questions such as the above take the reader **out** of the printed page into the depths of the mind to analyze, reason, and find information necessary for responding appropriately to the question. Students also seem to enjoy the real-life types of questions. These help make it easier to transfer this same skill into printed matter.

SECTION C:
THE WRITTEN QUESTION

A variety of written questions may be prepared for the purpose of building the comprehension skill of prediction or projection. The following are some samples.

> *The police arrived just as Rebecca was about to pull the trigger. How might this story have ended if the police had waited two more minutes before they left for Rebecca's house?*

The above style of question ("What might have happened if....") should be used carefully. That which follows the word **if** is often insignificant. "What might have happened if the boy had had blue eyes instead of brown?" is an example of such an absurdity.

Also consider the differences in the wording of such question stems. The words **might, would, could,** and **should** can be crucial choices in such questions. Ponder the difference in "What **might** have happened when the alarm sounded?" and "What **should** have happened when the alarm sounded?"

> *Read to the bottom of page 24, then stop. Predict the outcome of this story.*

The above type of question is frequently asked, but it should be used with great caution. Consider for a moment one bright young erudite child who **accurately** predicts what is actually going to happen! Now what? Did you ever hear what the ending of a novel was going to be while you were in the middle of it? Another consideration: Does every class member finish reading to the bottom of page 24 at the **same time?** What happens to those who get there first? Last? What about the possibility of a child who *has already read* the selection previously?

> *The story "Endless Journey" in RICK'S MONTHLY WORLD will not conclude until next issue. Based on the information given in the last four issues, try to predict how the story will end. Write your prediction on the provided 3" x 5" card and place it in the back of your science text. After next month's magazine arrives, read the conclusion of the story—then find your card to see how close your prediction was.*

> *The story you have just read will be Chapter 3 in a book entitled Jerry's Vacation. Write the title of Chapter 4 and also write the first paragraph for this chapter.*

GA1144

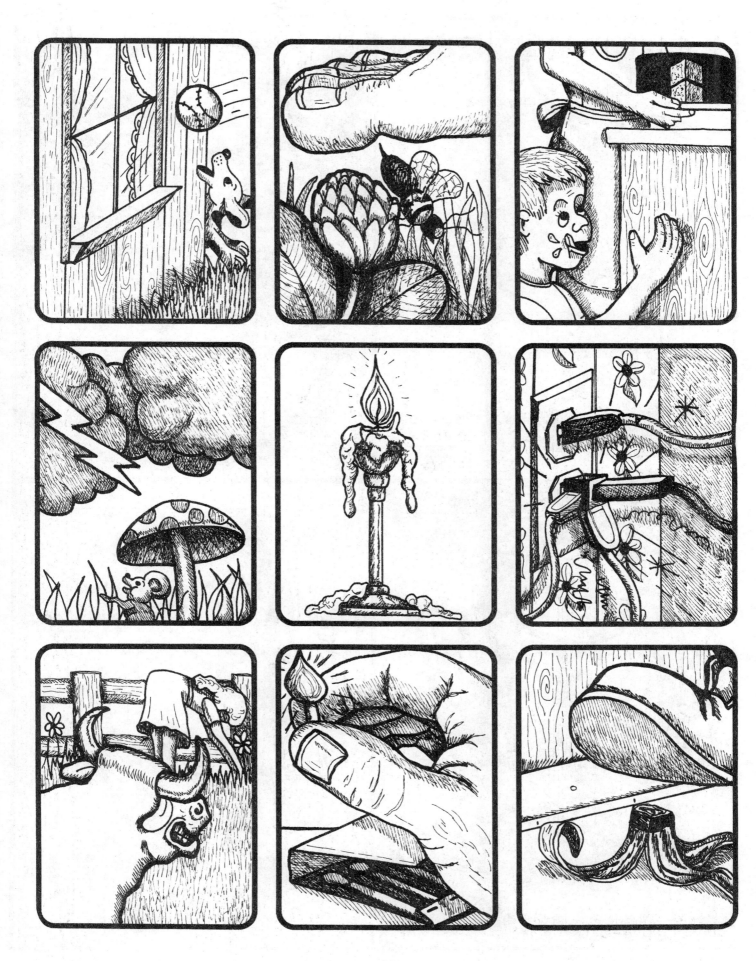

98

TEACHING
THE COMPREHENSION SUBSKILL OF UNDERSTANDING

WORDS OR PHRASES

Without knowledge of the meanings of individual words or phrases very little could be comprehended in a reading passage. The following sections describe various ways which vocabulary skills may be taught.

SECTION A:
VOCABULARY SKILLS

Vocabulary skills may be studied through an analysis of its individual subskills.

Synonyms are words which have similar meanings. Examples: *Funny, humorous; sad, sorrowful.*

Antonyms are words which have opposite or near opposite meanings. Examples: *Boy, girl; night, day.*

Homophones are words which are pronounced the same but have different spellings and meanings. Examples: *See, sea; to, two, too.*

Homographs are words which are spelled alike but which have different meanings and occasionally different pronunciations. Examples: *Run, turkey, bank, wind, record.*

Phrases may sometimes have meanings as a phrase rather than the combined meanings of the individual words. Examples: *"Buy a pig in a poke,"* or *"Cold as a cucumber."*

Word structure can frequently aid in determining the meaning of words. Any attention to the structure of the word will aid in this skill. This may be the roots, prefixes, suffixes, compound words, or syllables.

Individual word meanings will sometimes have to be taught because there is no other "group" in which they can be placed. These words may be taught through creative games.

GA1144

The above skills may be taught in a variety of different ways. Below are some examples.

The author of this story stated that Sharon could never be called haughty. In fact she was generally quite _____. Find this word which describes Sharon. Is this word a synonym, antonym, homophone, or a homograph for **haughty?** _____

The word **heart** *has many meanings. It is used in the fifth paragraph of this story. Find the word and consider its meaning in this reading selection. Which of the following is it?*
_____ *A. An organ which pumps blood*
_____ *B. The center of something*
_____ *C. Etc.*

In the third paragraph of this story is a word which means **friendly.** *Find and write this word.*

In this story Jim was called an **infracaninophile.** *Using the context of the paragraph in which this word was used or examining the meanings of the individual word parts, try to determine the meaning of this word. Then check your dictionary for accuracy.*

SECTION B:
CREATIVE VOCABULARY ACTIVITIES

In addition to the above study of vocabulary subskills, word meanings may be taught via several creative or game exercises. The following are some examples.

Crossword puzzles may be prepared in many different ways. They may be as simple as only two intersecting words or they may be quite complex.

Several computer software programs offer easy ways for students themselves to prepare such puzzles. These puzzles may also be prepared to fit inside an outline of an object which is significant to the reading selection (such as the outline of a baseball).

Word search puzzles are generally enjoyed by readers of all ages. These may be prepared by first identifying a list of words pertinent to the reading selection. The letters to these words may then be placed in a grid and spelled forwards, backwards, upside down, and diagonally. Do consider giving learners a list of words to be found. When possible, try to attach **meanings** for these words in order to avoid an exercise of visual discrimination without thought.

Anagrams may create interest in the study of selected words in a passage. Anagrams are words or phrases made by transposing the letters of other words or phrases. The following is a sample question.

The word **read** *is an anagram for a word found in this selection which was used to address the man's wife. What was this word?*

Other word puzzles such as alphabet codes, word scrambles, etc., may be used to challenge learners in the study of word and phrase meanings. Encourage students to create vocabulary activities and games which may be worked by their classmates.

GA1144

TEACHING
THE COMPREHENSION SUBSKILL OF
NOTING
OTHER SIGNIFICANT

Details have sometimes been described as the "trivia" of the passage. In many cases they are "facts" such as Who, What, When, Where, etc.

Detail questions may be literal if they are stated in the passage or they may be inferred. Some details are important; others are simply annoying if they have to be memorized for an examination or discussion. This skill is likely to be the most frequently **used** and **abused** skill of all the comprehension tasks. Because some detail questions are so quick to prepare and generally so obviously "right" or "wrong," sometimes there tends to be an OVERLOAD of detail questions.

Inexperienced question-writers tend to write "Who did . . .?" "Where did . . . happen?" "How many . . .?" "Which one . . .?" "What color was the . . .?" as a **complete** measure of comprehension. Lack of training and thought in such question-designing may gradually lead students to erroneously believe that *finding details* and *passage comprehension* are synonymous. Of course, they are not. In a 20-question collection of comprehension questions, one or two items should involve locating the facts. The remainder should be more diversified and, perhaps, more thought-provoking than the "typical" fact-finding task.

The following sections provide information and samples regarding this type of question.

SECTION A: NOTING DETAILS THROUGH PICTURES

For early learners the examination of pictures may provide special training in noting details, whether literal or inferred. For total nonreaders a picture without a story may be shown. Questions may be prepared to measure the learner's interpretation of the details shown in the pictures. Pages 103-106 provide examples of this type of activity. Two full page pictures are provided each with a multitude of details drawn. Each picture is followed by a set of detail questions. Not all of these questions need to be used. The list of questions begins with the easiest to answer and proceeds to the more inferential and difficult. Use only those which match the needs of the learners involved. Additional pictures may be prepared from other sources, if desired.

For beginning readers pictures may be correlated with a brief reading passage in order to teach details. Learners are asked to read the selection, examine the provided picture, and note the **mismatches** with the picture and the script. Pages 107-110 are examples of pictures and passages which may be used in this manner. The instructor may choose to read aloud the selection then show the picture, or the picture may be in view **while** the selection is being read. Note that these two different techniques develop different types of skills.

SECTION B:
THE WRITTEN QUESTION

Before writing a detail question, ask the following questions:

1) Just what are the **significant details** in this selection?

2) With which of these details should the students be concerned?

3) How can this concern be generated?

Always be cautious when writing detail questions. The following questions will demonstrate this need.

What was the third word in the fourth paragraph?

Some detail questions actually have about as much significance as the above question. Be cautious to insure that the answer is **worth** the learner's time!

How many characters were in "The Three Little Pigs"?

Consider possible confusion with such a question. Besides, is this important?

Who was the main character in the story "Eric"?

Might the above question be subject to the reader's opinion? Might it also be the title?

Consider the value of the following ques-

tions with regard to forcing the reader to think carefully about the passage.

(Passage: ". . .Teddy walked from his front porch toward his mail box. He couldn't wait to see if Susan had written. In his haste, he almost slipped on the icy sidewalk. He cautionsly. . .") *What season of the year was it in this story?*

(Passage: ". . . Mary hastened to her car. The darkness sent chills through her entire body. Neither of the cars in the parking lot could be seen clearly. She knew which was hers, though, because . . .) How many cars were in the parking lot besides Mary's? (The answer is prominent in the mystery's solution.)

The following pictures show Larky's three positions in "Larky's Luck." Draw lines from the picture to the corresponding description of a story event.

Larky—while anticipating Kan's visit.
Larky—while Kan is talking with him.
Larky—after hearing Kan's message.

GA1144

104

Detail Questions for "Dad's Delight"

Below are detail questions which may be used with the picture entitled "Dad's Delight." The first questions are simpler and more literal. The final questions are more inferential in nature and require a higher level of thinking skills. Use only those which fit the level and abilities of the learners. The picture may be held in view while the questions are being read and answered, or it may be given to the learners to study and then withdrawn while the questions are asked. All answers are provided, although the wording of such answers may take many forms. Additional questions may be prepared, if desired.

What household chore is the man doing? (Washing dishes, because the water is running.)

What live animals are showing? (A cat and dog. The mouse is only a toy.)

Is the dog allowed indoors? (Likely yes because a dog bone is on the floor.)

Is the cat allowed indoors? (Likely yes because of the toy mouse.)

What time is it? (8:15)

Is it morning or evening? (Evening, because it is dark outside. Although it *can* be dark in some places at 8:15 in the morning, it would not likely be this dark.)

Is the light turned on or off? (It is turned on. There are two clues: the light switch, and the visibility of things inside at night.)

Of the four seasons, which one is it? (Winter)

The winter season can have different kinds of weather. What was this day's likely forecast? (Snow!)

How long has it been snowing? (At least 30 minutes or longer because the snow has accumulated on the branches of the tree.)

Of the holiday seasons, which one is it? (Christmas, because of the holly.)

How many children likely live in this house? (At least two.)

Are these children boys or girls? (The younger one is probably a girl because of the lace around the bib. The older one is probably a boy because of a baseball bat. Although this bat could belong to the father or to a girl who is also interested in baseball, the name "John" on the math paper on the wall is a clue.)

How old are these children? (The younger one is about one or two years old because of the high chair and the baby rattle on the floor. The older one is likely six or seven. The clues to the latter are the bat and the math paper on the wall.)

What will John's grade likely be in math for this semester? (It could be anything; however, he is probably an average math student since he missed only one problem on the paper on the wall. The grade on this paper is a "B." This does not necessarily indicate that his grade will be the same on his report card.)

How does this man feel about washing dishes? (He is probably not thrilled. The expression on his face fails to show sheer delight!)

Does this man want to get "dishpan hands"? (Likely not because he is wearing a plastic glove.)

Is this man right-handed or left-handed? (He is likely left-handed because the gloved hand is his left. This, however, is not necessarily a true indication of handedness, although most people will glove their dominant hand.)

Does this man drink coffee? (He probably does since there is a coffee cup to be washed. However, other beverages are drunk in similar cups and others may have dined with him.)

The man is holding a broken plate. Why are there no pieces on the floor? (The plate likely broke in the sink and he has just noticed.)

What kinds of food were recently served? (At least an apple and a hot dog. The core of the apple is still on the counter and the hot dog is on the floor. There are no clues, however, regarding the food served on the unwashed dishes.)

How well can this man see? (He likely has

a vision problem since he does have glasses in his pocket. Perhaps he does not need them to wash dishes, but he might wear them if he sat down to read the newspaper.)

How much money does this man likely spend on clothes? (We really don't know. There is evidence only for those clothes he wears while he is washing dishes. His jeans have a patch on them and one of his shoes is worn out. However, when he goes to work, he may look like a million dollars! Who can tell?)

Where is the mother? (Again, we don't know. She could be in the next room filing her nails. She could be in the hospital having another baby. She could be on vacation. Or there might not be a mother living there at all.)

Detail Questions for "Patty's Pets"

Below are detail questions which may be used with the picture entitled "Patty's Pets." The first questions are simpler and more literal. The final questions are more inferential in nature and require a higher level of thinking skills. Use only those which fit the level and abilities of the learners. The picture may be held in view while the questions are being read and answered, or it may be given to the learners to study and then withdrawn while the questions are asked. All answers are provided, although the wording of such answers may take many forms. Additional questions may be prepared, if desired.

How old is Patty? (Judging from appearance, she is probably between twelve and sixteen. However, we all know the dangers of such judgments!)

What actions is she performing? (Both talking and writing.)

How many different live pets are in the picture? (Four—a mouse, a goldfish, a bird, and a dog.)

Will the dog in the picture run away? (It is possible since he is not on a leash. However, he may be the store's mascot and not try to get away.)

What might the dog's next action be? (He has spied the ball, so he may chase it and play with it.)

What has Patty likely eaten lately? (An apple, half a sandwich, and a bite from a cookie.)

How does Patty feel about pets? (She likely adores them. Clues: She is working in a pet shop, she has a poster and a T-shirt with positive messages, she is "wearing" a mouse, and she has a pleasant look on her face.)

If you bought two T-shirts at *Patty's Pets,* how much would you spend? (Six dollars plus tax.)

What pet might Patty have sold minutes earlier? (Likely a bird of some kind because of the feathers on the floor.)

If you telephoned *Patty's Pets,* what kind of answer would you get? (None, because the telephone is not plugged in.)

If you wanted to buy a snake, would you go to *Patty's Pets?* (Probably, because she has obvious information on snakes and might order one if she didn't have one in the store at the time.)

If you had a problem with your collie, would *Patty's Pets* be a good place to go? (It might, because Patty has a book on her shelf entitled *Collies.)*

Which would be a better place to be if you needed information on fish: *Patty's Pets* or your home? (Likely *Patty's Pets* unless your home has several books on fish.)

Would YOU want to work at *Patty's Pets?* (Answers will vary. Those interested in pets may wish to work there. Those not interested would likely not wish to do so.)

GA1144

SLEEPY SAM

Sam sat in the shade of an old oak tree. He was reading the newspaper. It was a warm, sunny day. Soon he became sleepy. He rested the newspaper against his motorcycle. He pulled his straw hat over his face. Before long he was sound asleep.

Below is a picture of this scene at the end. However, some things do not fit the words for the story. Make a list of every detail in the picture which does not match the words above.

GA1144

THE PICNIC

Mary's family went on a picnic. Each person in her family had a job to do. It was Mary's job to spread out the food.

Mary first placed a white tablecloth on the ground. It was a windy day. The edges of the cloth began flapping in the breeze. She found a large rock to hold down one corner of the cloth. She put the heavy picnic basket on the other.

She opened the basket. She took out the sandwiches and put them beside the picnic basket. Next she placed a large bag of chips. Mary couldn't resist. She opened the bag of chips and ate a few. She put some apples by the chips. She put a box of cookies by the apples.

She put a gallon of lemonade beside the tablecloth. She put the paper cups near the lemonade. She went back to the car and brought a large watermelon. She sliced it into eight pieces.

By now there was no room left on the cloth for the napkins, plates and forks. So she spread out a towel and put them on it.

Mary now had the food ready. She left to find the rest of her family. While she was gone, the wind blew away all but two napkins. An apple rolled off the cloth. A leaf fell onto the top plate. Five big ants began crawling up the side of the picnic basket. Several wasps began flying around the spout of the lemonade jug. A little dog dragged away the whole box of cookies.

Do you think Mary was happy when she returned?

On a separate page is a picture of this scene at the end. However, some things do not fit the descriptions in the above story. Make a list of every detail in the picture which does not match the words above.

109

Answers for "Sleepy Sam"

After reading the "Sleepy Sam" aloud, show the picture and ask learners to identify any differences in the words which were read and the details shown in the picture. The following is a list of some of these differences:

- Sam is lying flat on the ground instead of sitting.
- He is not in the shade of the tree.
- The tree is not an oak tree.
- He was reading a book instead of a newspaper.
- He has a bicycle instead of a motor-cycle.
- He does not have a straw hat.

Answers for "The Picnic"

After reading the "The Picnic" aloud, show the picture and ask learners to identify any differences in the words which were read and the details shown in the picture. The following is a list of some of these differences:

- The tablecloth is not white. It is checkered.
- There is no large rock holding down one corner of the cloth.
- The tablecloth is not square as was implied with the word *corner*. It is round.
- The bag of chips has not been opened.
- There are no apples by the chips (or anywhere at all).
- The box of cookies has been opened and is still on the tablecloth. (The dog was supposed to have dragged it away.)
- The lemonade pitcher is not a full gallon. The measurements on it indicate that it is likely only three quarts.
- The cups by the lemonade appear to be glass instead of paper.
- The watermelon has been sliced into only six pieces instead of eight.
- The forks are on the tablecloth instead of the towel.
- Knives and spoons are also on the tablecloth.
- There are three napkins left instead of only two.
- There is no fallen leaf on the top plate.
- There are more than five ants crawling on the picnic basket.
- There are butterflies instead of wasps flying around the lemonade.
- The lemonade is not in a jug.
- The lemonade container does not have a spout.

GA1144

TEACHING ADDITIONAL COMPREHENSION SUBSKILLS OF

All of the previously described subskills may be inferential in nature. Although some of them involve only a literal interpretation of the printed material (such as the subskill of details), the majority of the questions prepared may (and should) request the reader to "read between the lines."

Several of these subskills may be combined into one question. Good comprehension questions need not teach **just one** subskill at a time. Below are some examples.

SECTION A: ADDITIONAL COMPREHENSION SUBSKILLS

Several comprehension subskills may be taught in addition to those in the previous sections. The following questions demonstrate some of these.

*There were four characters in this story. These characters were of quite different sizes. On the measuring chart below, the letter **B** appears to show how tall Balboa is. The letter **S** shows Steve's height. Draw a **P** where Pinky might be, and a **J** where Jason might be.*

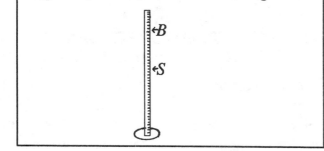

The story for the above question never indicated the height of *any* of the characters. The learner must remember clues such as *"Steve stared down at Pinky. . . ."* or *"Jason reached up and grasped Balboa's hand."*

Pictured below are two objects mentioned in the story. Study these carefully, then tell two ways these objects are alike and two ways they are different.

*After reading the chapter on the early American settlers, consider the difficulties these people had as they were determined to proceed westward through the new land. Their methods of transportation were quite different from those we have today. List four transportation problems which they likely had at that time which we would **not** have today. Explain your choices. List four transportation problems which **we might** have today which they **could not** have had at that time. Next list four transportation problems which might occur three hundred years from now.*

GA1144

The preceding question encompasses both the subskills of comparison/contrast and prediction (discussed in a previous section).

> *Picture in your mind the expression on Pam's face when she first heard that her sister had been in an accident. Now picture her face when she received the news that her sister was not hurt. How are these two faces different?*

The above question may be used by having volunteers "show" these faces.

> *In this story Jim felt that old Mrs. Watson was not fair to him. He felt that she liked his brother George better because she gave George twelve cookies and gave him only six. However, he forgot to consider the size of these cookies. In the space provided draw the twelve cookies Mrs. Watson gave to George. Then draw the six cookies she gave to Jim. How do they compare in total amount?*
> *George's cookies:*
>
>
> *Jim's cookies:*

Many of the above questions teach the comprehension subskill of comparisons/contrasts. Many are mixed with other comprehension subskills presented in previous sections. Below is a question which teaches the subskill of cause and effect.

> *The picture shown below shows a happening in the story. Draw the effects of this picture in the blank box.*
>

SECTION B: THE EXIT QUESTION

An exit question is one which causes the student to consider material found in a source **other than** the one which has just been read or heard. Consider the following samples.

> *In the story "The Three Little Pigs" a wolf was trying to capture the little pigs for his lunch. Think of three other stories in which a wolf caused others to fear for their lives. Name these stories and tell what happened to the wolf in each one.*

> *The python in this story was trying to swallow a baby elephant. The python was described as being thirty feet in length. Is it possible for a thirty-foot python to actually swallow a baby elephant? Look in your science book or check in a reference book to find out the largest animal a python has been known to swallow. Find out how much a baby elephant weighs at birth. With this information, determine whether or not a python could actually swallow a baby elephant.*

Note that the above question encompasses the subskills of prediction, comparisons, and reality—in addition to engaging the learner in examining outside sources for accuracy of information presented.

SECTION B: CORRELATING COMPREHENSION WITH CREATIVE DRAMATICS

A method to encompass a variety of comprehension skills, especially the inference skills, is to correlate creative dramatics activities with the story. The following are some examples.

> *In the story "The Three Bears" Goldilocks ran away at the end. She thought about what she had done to the bears and decided to go back and apologize. She is now knocking at the door. Find three of your friends and enact this conversation.*

The above questions force learners to examine the character traits of each character in addition to considering all of the verbal content choices and the verbal delivery choices for such an exercise.

> *One scene in the story "The Rabbit and the Fox" tells about how the rabbit tricked the fox. This scene has much action. Find a friend and demonstrate this active scene.*

SECTION C:
CORRELATING COMPREHENSION WITH CREATIVE EXPRESSION

Creative expression may be either oral or written. Both should be included as much as possible. Creative expression may be correlated with the comprehension skills by having the speakers or writers reflect upon the information in the passage then prepare a verbal response. The following are some samples.

> *The third little pig wants to write a letter home to his mother and tell her about what has happened to all three of her children. Write (or tell) what this letter might say.*

Regarding the above question, three different students might write *three* different letters—one from each of the three little pigs. An interesting **contrast** of these letters might be made.

> *Chad had an exciting adventure when he tried to sleep in the forest. If he later writes his autobiography, he might include this adventure as a chapter. Write (or tell) this chapter.*

> *In the story "Snow White" the wicked stepmother fell down dead at the end of the story. The local newspaper heard of her death and wanted to write an obituary. You have been asked to write this obituary. What will you say?*

The above question may also involve exit information. For those students who have not read an obituary, samples may need to be located as models.

SECTION D: USING CARTOONS TO TEACH COMPREHENSION SKILLS

Selected cartoons may be used to teach the comprehension skill of inference (and other specific comprehension skills). Pages 114-116 provide examples for this purpose. Cartoons numbered 1-5 have no words to read for the cartoon intrepretation. These may be used with nonreaders (or with readers). Cartoons 6-12 contain a few words which are necessary for the interpretation. Should these be used with nonreaders, the words may be read to the learners in advance or each cartoon may be used one at a time with a group.

The instructional leader may ask learners to explain the meaning or humor of the cartoon. A group discussion may occur regarding these interpretations. If written responses are desired, separate paper may be used.

The daily newspapers provide multitudes of additional cartoons which may be used for this purpose. Students may also draw examples.

INFERENCE CARTOON 1

INFERENCE CARTOON 2

INFERENCE CARTOON 3

INFERENCE CARTOON 4

114

GA1144

INFERENCE CARTOON 5

INFERENCE CARTOON 6

INFERENCE CARTOON 7

INFERENCE CARTOON 8

INFERENCE CARTOON 9

INFERENCE CARTOON 10

INFERENCE CARTOON 11

INFERENCE CARTOON 12

GA1144

TEACHING
THE COMPREHENSION SUBSKILL OF

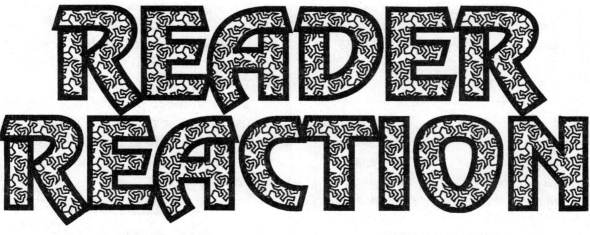

RESPONSE AND JUDGMENT

An often overlooked comprehension skill is that of allowing and encouraging the reader to **react** or **respond** or **make judgments** regarding what has been read. Since many of these questions have no "right" or "wrong" answer, some teachers choose to ignore them altogether. However, building these skills in the *affective* dimension of learning can be as crucial in many cases as those in the cognitive.

The following sections provide suggestions regarding the development of this comprehension skill.

SECTION A: USING FACE PICTURES

Page 120 provides four pictures of common reactions to information (being *angry*, *sad*, *happy*, or *unconcerned*). This page may be used in a variety of different ways. One method is to duplicate the page for each student. The four duplicated pictures may be cut out and placed on ice cream sticks for learners to hold in the air in response to selected questions such as the following examples.

> *Think about how you would have felt if you had been the Wee Small Bear when he discovered that his chair had been broken by Goldilocks? Look at the four faces in front of you. Hold up the one which best shows how you think he might have felt.*

> *The story "Dog Gone" leaves readers with many different feelings. How did you feel at the end of the story? Hold up the face which best shows this feeling.*

The above questions are to be used with pictures found on page 120. More pictures may be used. Fourteen smaller pictures are provided on the "Reader Response Card" shown on the following page. These may be duplicated and placed on work sheets, exam copies, or task

GA1144

cards for a more in-depth response to how readers feel or how they consider various characters to have felt at different points in a story. The following are some sample questions.

> *Write the number of the picture on the Reader Response Card which best shows how you felt after you read "The Mouse and the Frog." _____*
> *Tell why you felt this way.*

> *At the beginning of this story, you likely had a different feeling than you did at the end. Which number shows how you felt at the beginning and which shows how you felt at the end?*
> *Beginning? _____*
> *End? _____*
> *Explain each of your choices.*

A variety of different types of questions or responses may occur with these fourteen pictures. Consider a question such as the following.

> *Look at the face pictured by number 8. Can you think of a time you have felt like this? Explain your answer.*

Each of the faces on the Reader Response Card could be used in the above fashion. This type of question lends itself best to oral discussion, especially when the skill is first introduced to learners.

These fourteen pictures may be photocopied for use as finger puppets. Learners may attach these puppets to their fingers to show reactions as stories are being told. The learners may also suggest other uses.

SECTION B:
CHARACTER BADGES
AND SIGNS

Pages 121-124 may be used for a variety of reader reaction activities. Below are some examples.

YOU BE THE JUDGE! Using the badges shown on pages 121-122, students may select a badge for each main character in the story they

READER RESPONSE CARD

1 2 3 4 5 6 7

8 9 10 11 12 13 14

118

GA1144

have just read or heard. This activity overlaps with the skill of determining character traits because it is necessary to determine both the traits of the characters and to make a judgment regarding their actions. Several approaches could be taken with this activity. One might be to indicate that others need to be "warned" about the behavior of a particular character. This warning may occur by having that character wear a badge to indicate what others might need to know.

Should appropriate messages not appear on those provided, an extra half page of blank ones may be used to prepare additional ones.

Sign out! The signs appearing on pages 123-124 may be used for readers to express their feelings following the reading of or listening to a specific selection. Several generic ones are presented on these pages. A large blank one appears to be used to write any message desired by the reader. Index cards may be prepared in the same manner.

SECTION C:
THE WRITTEN QUESTION

A variety of written questions may be prepared for this skill. The following are some examples.

---

*In "Brian's Pets" Brian had a difficult time when his pet died. Have **you** ever had a pet die? If so, how did you feel? Did you react in the same way Brian did?*

---

*Which word best describes how **you** felt at the end of "The Rabbit's Adventure"?*
(A) RELIEVED, because . . .
(B) ANGRY, because. . .
(C) SAD, because. . .

---

*In "David's Game" David was allowed to continue in his mean treatment to his little brother. Do **you** think this should have been allowed? Explain why you feel as you do.*

The author of "Mr. Fox and the Turkey" pointed out many of Mr. Fox's good qualities. However, he mentioned only a few of the Turkey's. Do you think that he treated them both fairly in his story? Explain your answer.

How did you feel when the author used the expression "a wicked brother" as he described Joe? Tell why you felt this way.

In "My Father's Store" Bev took many items from her father's store without paying for them or telling anyone she had taken them. Do you feel this is acceptable since she was the store owner's daughter? Do you think this was really stealing? Tell why you feel as you do.

---

*In "The Wicked Animal" a wolf did some bad things to many of the other animals. Is it all right to mistreat others if we are stronger and bigger? Do you think it would be all right for **you** to do some of these same things to some of your classmates and friends? Explain your answer.*

GA1144

120

GA1144

May I help you?

Come closer! I may be able to steal something from you! Eh, eh!

I talk to strangers!

If it isn't going to help me, then why bother?

Good morning! Isn't it a wonderful day?

I'm bigger than you, so I'll do as I please.

At your service!

Don't mess with me!

Get out of my way or I'll punch your lights out!

Nobody's watching, so let's take it!

I'm the face rearranger!

I trust everybody!

GA1144

Be careful.
I'm sneaky!

I'm precious,
but I'm
dumb.

Hit me and
I'll cry!

I'm foxier
than you!

We only live
once, so let's
have fun!

If you hurt
anyone in
my family,
I'll get
even.

Write your own.

122

GA1144

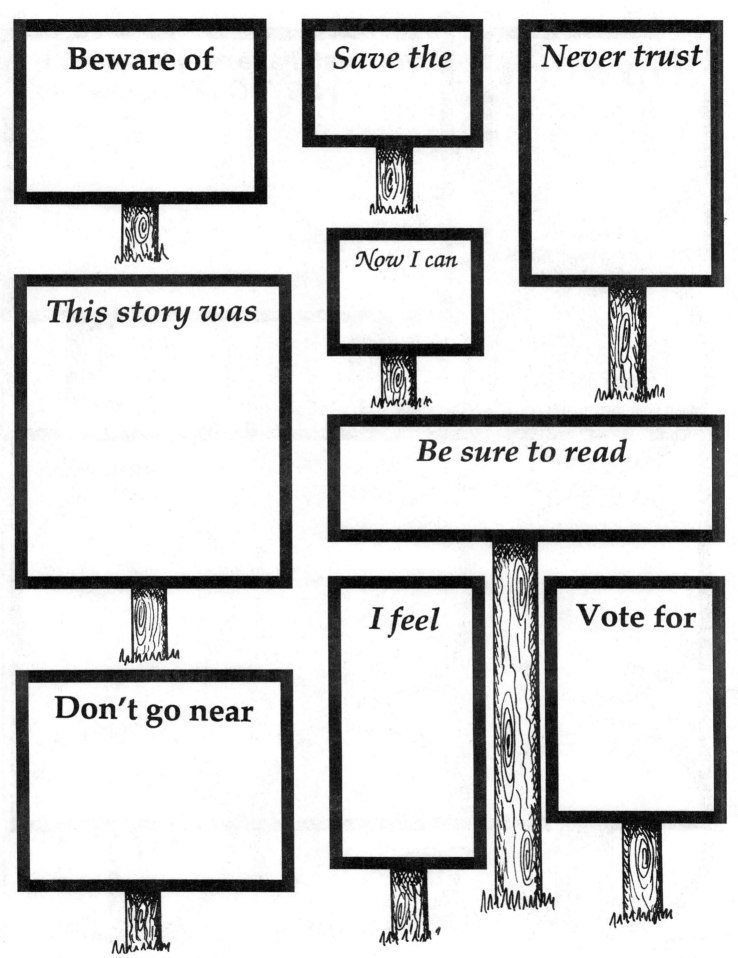

Beware of

Save the

Never trust

This story was

Now I can

Be sure to read

Don't go near

I feel

Vote for

GA1144

Up with

Now that I have read this story I want EVERYBODY to know that

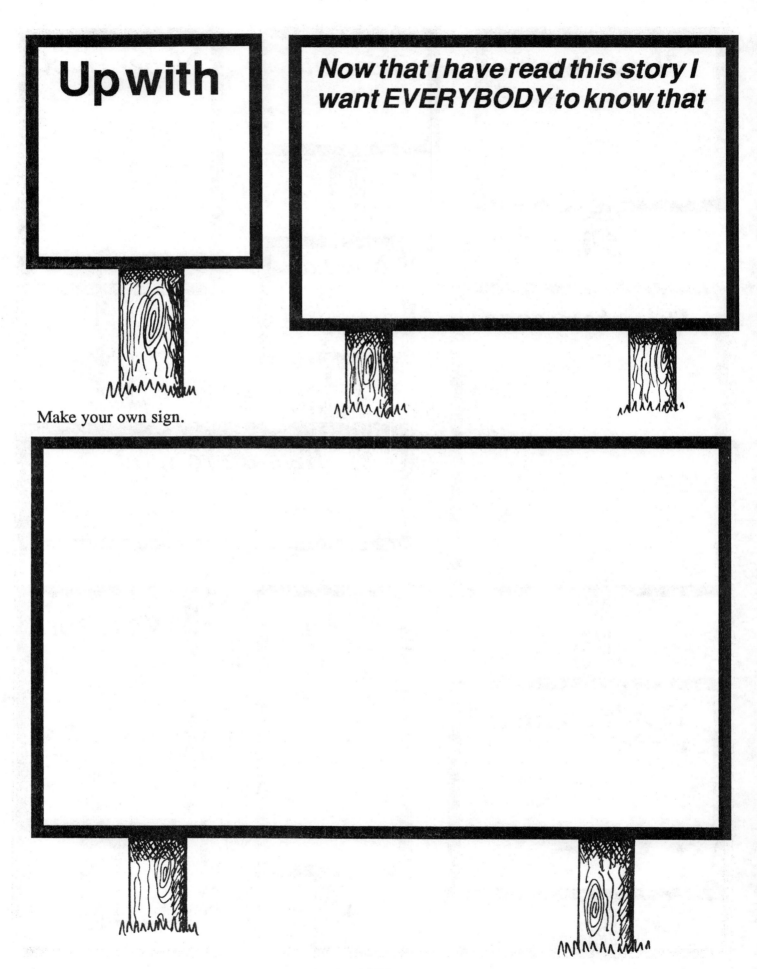

Make your own sign.

Part 2

INSTRUCTIONAL OBJECTIVES FOR PART 2

Part 2 is a section which demonstrates how the textual material presented in Part 1 may be practically applied in a classroom or tutorial situation. All of the skills discussed in Part 1 may be used with any reading selection which is intended for readers in the primary or elementary grades. Thousands of possibilities of variations of exercises, activities, and individual questions may be presented.

This section uses a well-known children's story, "The Wolf and the Seven Little Goats," to demonstrate one application of these skills. These exercises and activities may be photocopied and distributed to individual learners. If desired, they may be prepared in permanent reusable fashion by laminating or protecting each page with clear self-adhesive paper. If the latter is chosen, it is still recommended that each student be supplied with a consumable copy of pages 134-135. For these two activities, it is difficult to transfer the answers onto separate paper. It is recommended that pages 140-141 be photocopied and stapled to several blank pages to form a creative writing booklet for those learners who can write. For those with extra energy, these pages may be trimmed at the outside border of the design for creative shape booklets. Page 127 may be used as a learning center backdrop for the prepared materials. Page 128 is a copy of the story.

The instructional objectives for each activity are as follows:

Page 129: The learner will accurately determine at least five of the differences in written version of the story as compared with the pictured version.

Page 130: The learner will accurately identify the pictured story character and determine the corresponding part in the story which this picture fits.

Page 131: The learner will write a theme sentence for each main character in the story. This sentence may either reflect the main idea (as it relates to that character) or it may be a clever motto which relates to character traits.

Page 132: The learner will accurately match pictorial representations of causes and effects as they relate to this story.

Page 133: The learner will accurately determine whether pictures represent reality or fantasy ideas.

Page 134: The learner will accurately draw lines (straight and/or curved) to depict the order of events of the wolf in the story.

Page 135: The learner will accurately select and write words from the story which correspond to their provided meanings.

Page 136: The learner will write an appropriate main idea as it relates to the lesson learned by the wolf in this story.

Page 137: The learner will identify characters from other stories and compare them with a similar character in this story.

Page 138: The learner will match a word to a pictured character demonstrating the meaning of that word.

Page 139: The learner will accurately pronounce (and use contextually in a sentence) selected words from the story.

Pages 140-141: The learner will write (or tell) an appropriate continuation to a story beginning.

Page 142: The learner will portray the actions of selected characters in the story by performing in situational skits.

GA1144

The Wolf and the Seven Little Goats

On the table below are several exciting activities for the story "The Wolf and the Seven Little Goats." Select those which you wish to work and return them to the table when you have finished. An answer card is available for those pages with specific written responses. Have fun as you do these activities!

GA1144

The Wolf and the Seven Little Goats

Rewritten by Flora Joy

Once there was a mother goat who had seven little goats. One day she had to leave their house to get food for them to eat. Before she left, she warned them not to let anyone in while she was gone.

"The wicked wolf will see me leave. He will try to get inside the house so he can have all of you for his dinner! You must not let him in," the mother goat warned.

"Do not worry, mother, dear.
We'll let no one in when you're not here!"

The mother goat left her house with peace of mind.

Shortly thereafter, there was a knock at the door.

"Open the door, my children. This is your mother and I have brought some food for you to eat," said someone at the door.

"You're not our mother with food to eat.
Your voice is hoarse, but hers is sweet!"

The angry wolf stalked away from the house. He went to the store and bought a pound of marshmallows. He ate them to make his voice soft. He returned to the goats' house.

"Open the door, my children. This is your mother and I have brought some food for you to eat," he said in a soft voice.

"We won't let you in until
You've placed your paws upon the sill."

When the wolf placed his paws on the window-sill, the little goats cried out,

"You're just a wolf who wants a snack!
Our mother has no paws that black!"

The angry wolf went to a paint store and bought a can of white paint. As soon as he was out of sight, he opened the can of paint and dipped his paws in it. They soon dried.

Once more he returned to the goats' home. "Open the door, my children. This is your mother and I have brought some food for you to eat," he said in a soft voice as he placed his paws on the windowsill for them to see.

The seven little goats were fooled by this ploy and they let the wolf in. As soon as they did, they realized he was the wicked wolf. They all ran and hid.

The wolf chuckled as he walked through the house to find them. He found the first little goat under the bed and swallowed him whole. He found the second little goat behind a door and swallowed him whole. He found the third beneath the staircase, the fourth under the table, the fifth in a cabinet, and the sixth behind a chair. He swallowed each one whole, all except for the seventh little goat who hid in a large butter churn.

The wolf, no longer hungry, went back to his home and fell asleep.

Soon the mother goat came home. How frightened she was at what she saw. She called out to each of her little goats one at a time. On the seventh call, she heard a voice say,

"Oh, what a shock on your return
To find me in the butter churn."

She quickly pulled the little goat out of the butter churn and he told her what had happened. They both raced to the wolf's house and found him in a deep sleep. Quietly, the mother goat took out her scissors and cut open the wolf's stomach. With a snip and a snap, the first little goat popped out. One at a time they jumped out alive and well, for the wolf had swallowed them whole. Each little goat gathered several large stones and placed them in the wolf's stomach. The mother goat quickly sewed the wolf's stomach back together.

Later when the wolf awoke, he was thirsty. He went to the water's edge and leaned over to get a drink. The weight of the stones caused him to topple into the water and drown.

The little goats, who were hiding in the bushes, saw what happened. All at once they danced and sang,

"A softer voice and whiter paws
Caused us to be misled.
But now we dance with joy because
The wicked wolf is dead!"

GA1144

Inside the Goats' House

The scene below shows how the goats' house looked as soon as the seven little goats ran to hide from the wolf. Several details, however, are not accurate. See how many of these details you can find. Write them on separate paper. After you finish, check the answer card to see how many you were able to find.

129

GA1144

Let's Face It!

Below are several pictures of goat faces. These are faces of either the mother goat or one of the seven little goats at some point in the story. Look closely at each picture. Decide which goat it is and in which part of the story the goat looked this way. Write your answers on separate paper. When you finish, compare your answers with those given on the answer card.

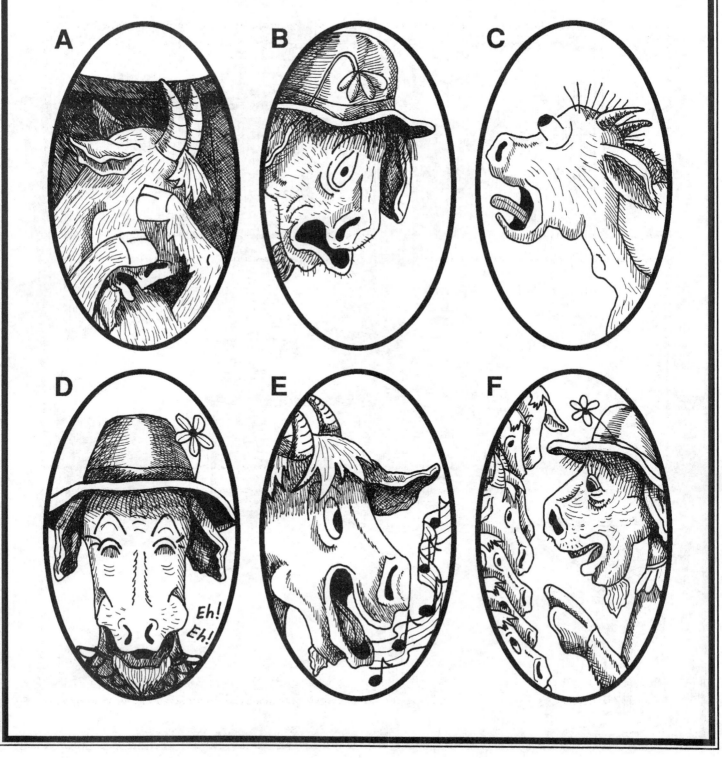

130

GA1144

Bumper Stickers

The mother goat is now driving a goatmobile. The little goats have a goatcycle. The wolf is in a casket on wheels. All of them want a bumper sticker for their new vehicle. **YOU** write the words for these bumper stickers in the rectangles below. Let this message reflect what the characters might have been thinking at the end of the story. After you finish, compare your answers with some samples given on the answer card.

GA1144

No "Kid"-ding

The wolf in this story did many different things, each resulting in a different outcome. The pictures at the left show these actions (causes). The pictures on the right show the effects. On separate paper number from one to four. Write the letter of each effect by its cause. After you finish, check the answer card to see which of your answers are correct.

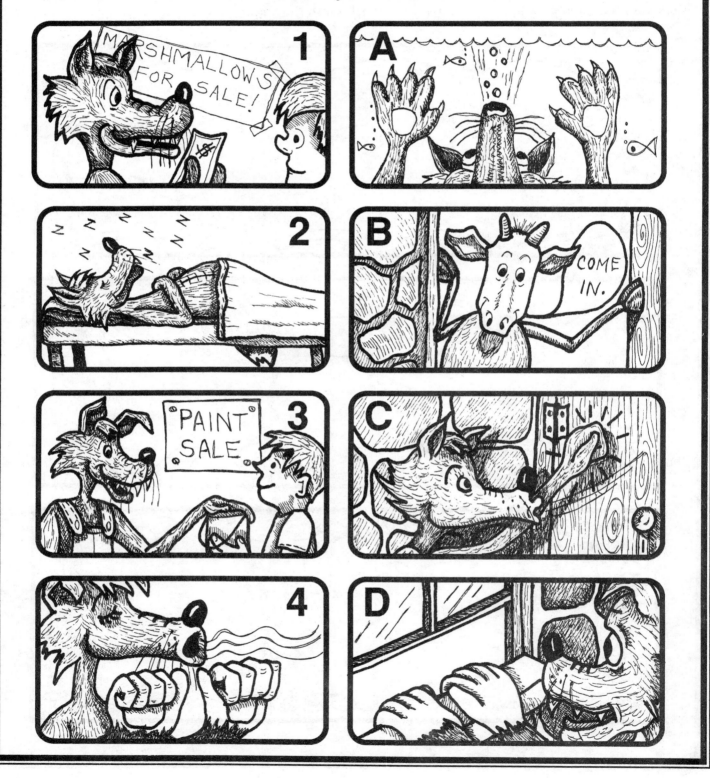

GA1144

Is It Real?

"The Wolf and the Seven Little Goats" is a fun story to read or tell. Is it true? **Could** it actually happen? Below are some pictures of some of the events in this story. On separate paper number from one to six. Write the word **YES** if the picture shows something from this story which **could** happen today. Write the word **NO** if the picture shows something which **could not** happen today. After you finish, check the answer card to see which of your answers are correct.

GA1144

The Wolf's Journey

The wolf went several different places in this story. The large X shows where the wolf was at the beginning of this story. Draw a line to show all of the places (in order) where the wolf went. When you finish, check the answer card to see if you were right.

134

CRAZY CROSSWORDS

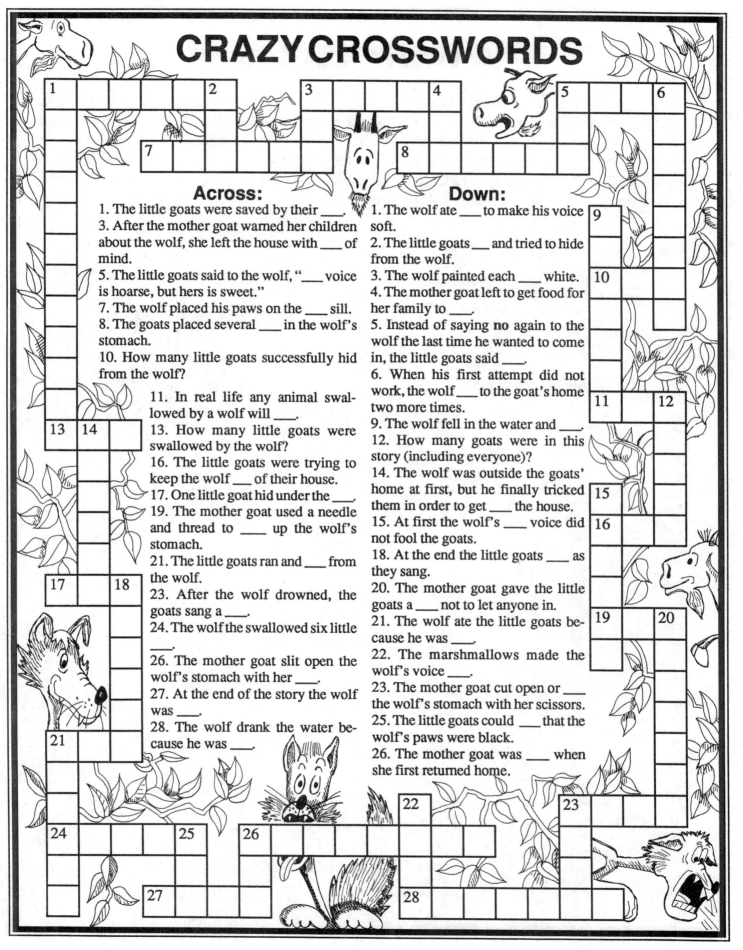

Across:

1. The little goats were saved by their ___.
3. After the mother goat warned her children about the wolf, she left the house with ___ of mind.
5. The little goats said to the wolf, "___ voice is hoarse, but hers is sweet."
7. The wolf placed his paws on the ___ sill.
8. The goats placed several ___ in the wolf's stomach.
10. How many little goats successfully hid from the wolf?
11. In real life any animal swallowed by a wolf will ___.
13. How many little goats were swallowed by the wolf?
16. The little goats were trying to keep the wolf ___ of their house.
17. One little goat hid under the ___.
19. The mother goat used a needle and thread to ___ up the wolf's stomach.
21. The little goats ran and ___ from the wolf.
23. After the wolf drowned, the goats sang a ___.
24. The wolf the swallowed six little ___.
26. The mother goat slit open the wolf's stomach with her ___.
27. At the end of the story the wolf was ___.
28. The wolf drank the water because he was ___.

Down:

1. The wolf ate ___ to make his voice soft.
2. The little goats ___ and tried to hide from the wolf.
3. The wolf painted each ___ white.
4. The mother goat left to get food for her family to ___.
5. Instead of saying **no** again to the wolf the last time he wanted to come in, the little goats said ___.
6. When his first attempt did not work, the wolf ___ to the goat's home two more times.
9. The wolf fell in the water and ___.
12. How many goats were in this story (including everyone)?
14. The wolf was outside the goats' home at first, but he finally tricked them in order to get ___ the house.
15. At first the wolf's ___ voice did not fool the goats.
18. At the end the little goats ___ as they sang.
20. The mother goat gave the little goats a ___ not to let anyone in.
21. The wolf ate the little goats because he was ___.
22. The marshmallows made the wolf's voice ___.
23. The mother goat cut open or ___ the wolf's stomach with her scissors.
25. The little goats could ___ that the wolf's paws were black.
26. The mother goat was ___ when she first returned home.

GA1144

A Grave Matter

The seven little goats learned a valuable lesson in this story. The wolf also learned a lesson. By the time he learned his lesson, however, it was too late. Some of his wolf friends heard about what happened to him, so they decided to write this lesson on his tombstone. Since wolf writing is invisible, **you** write the words for this lesson in the blank area on the stone below. There are many different correct ways to word this lesson. After you write what the wolf learned, compare your answer with the one provided on the answer card.

Shortcuts for Teaching Comprehension by Flora Joy, illustrated by Pat Harroll, © 1990 by Good Apple, Inc.,

Here lies
Mr. Wicked Wolf
who died while
learning this lesson:

GA1144

Wolves in Other Stories

The wolf is a popular character in children's stories. Think of other stories you have heard or read which have had a wolf in them. Were these wolves like the one in "The Wolf and the Seven Little Goats"? Consider the condition of each wolf at the end of these stories. Below are some pictures of these wolves. Do you remember the title for each of these stories? After you think about each one, compare your answers with those given on the answer card.

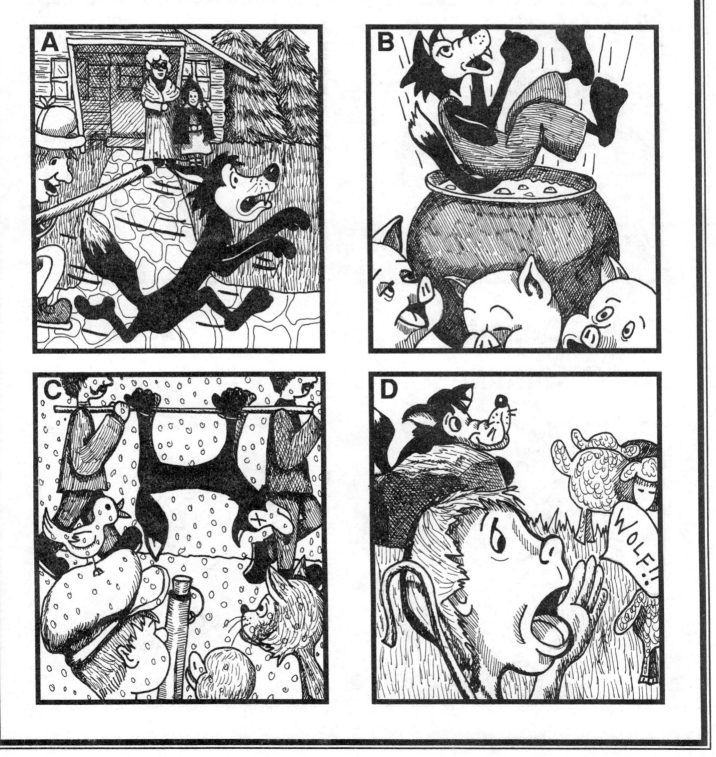

The Many Faces of the Wolf

The wolf had many different "faces" during this story. Below are four different pictures of these faces and four different words describing these faces. On separate paper number from one to four. Beside each number write the letter by the word which describes the picture. After you finish, check the answer card to see which of your answers are correct.

A. Deceitful
B. Expired
C. Satisfied
D. Angry

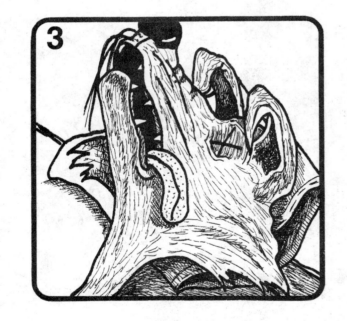

GA1144

Escape from the Wolf!

You are trying to escape from the wicked wolf. Beginning at the large **X**, start running through the path in the forest. However, there are several stones in your way. Each time you come to a stone, you may go around it **only** if you correctly pronounce the word on the stone and use it in a sentence. Each word on a stone was used in the story "The Wolf and the Seven Little Goats." If you miss as many as seven of these words, the wolf can pounce on you. If you do **not** miss more than seven before you arrive at the goats' house, you are safe forever! Happy traveling!

GA1144

Wolf Talk

You may not realize this, but all of us wolves **must** eat too, just the same as you must eat to stay alive. Wolves especially like little goats for supper. Had I been just a little smarter, I could have had a very nice meal that evening the mother goat played a trick on me. Here is my advice to the next wolf who approaches the goats' home. . . .

The Old Goat

The seventh little goat in this story grew up and had his own family. Years later his grandchildren asked him to tell them a story. He decided to tell them about the day the wolf got into their house when he was young. However, his memory is not very good, so many of the details have changed. Make up a story this goat might tell his grandchildren about that frightening day.

141

Acting Fun

"The Wolf and the Seven Little Goats" is filled with action. It can be fun being part of this action through skits. Below are some skits which you and your friends may enact.

Skit 1—Three Characters Needed: Cashier, Woman and Wolf

The wolf has gone to the grocery store to buy some marshmallows. He is standing in line to pay for them. A woman gets in line behind him and suddenly freaks out at seeing a wolf in a grocery store line buying marshmallows. A cashier is nearby. Enact this scene.

Skit 2—Several Wolves Needed

Mrs. Wolf returned home to find her dear husband drowned. She has called all of their relatives who are now gathered for the funeral. Enact this wolf funeral.

Skit 3—Eight Characters Needed: A Wolf and Seven Little Goats

About a month later a new wolf knocks on the door of the goat home while the mother goat is away. Enact this scene.

Skit 4—Two Characters Needed: A Store Clerk and a Wolf

The wolf is trying to buy some paint for his paws. The clerk, however, suspects that the wolf wants to use this paint in some way to harm some forest creatures. He doesn't want to sell the paint to the wolf. Enact this scene.

Skit 5—Nine Characters Needed: All Goats

The father goat has returned home after a long business trip. The mother goat tells him what happened and wants him to talk to the seven children. Enact this scene.

GA1144

ANSWER CARD

Inside the Goats' House

The bed in this picture is a water bed. A goat cannot hide beneath it. The goat in the picture is, therefore, on top of the bed. Another goat is on the stairs instead of beneath the staircase. Two goats are under the table instead of one. There is no little goat hiding behind a chair. The butter churn is full of milk instead of being empty. Even if it were empty, this churn is likely too small for the goat to crawl inside. The windowsill in this house might be too high for the wolf to reach with his paws. There is a window in the front door, and likely there would not have been one in the house in this story because the little goats could have looked through it to see who was there.

Let's Face It!

A. The seventh little goat is hiding inside the butter churn.
B. The mother goat has returned home to find that the wolf has eaten six of her children.
C. One of the little goats has just let the wolf inside their house.
D. The mother goat is pleased with what happened to the wolf at the end of the story.
E. A little goat is singing because the wolf has drowned and cannot harm them now.
F. The mother goat is warning her children not to let anyone in while she is away.

Bumper Stickers

There are many clever sentences for these bumper stickers. If you have trouble thinking of some, read the following: (Mother) This case is all sewed up! (Little Goats) Butt out of our lives! (Wolf) Don't drink while carrying stones!

Now try to think of some clever ones on your own.

No "Kid"-ding

1 is C; 2 is A; 3 is D; 4 is B.

Is It Real?

2, 3, and 6 are YES.

The Wolf's Journey

Lines which show the wolf's journey are drawn in the design at the right. Although your lines may be straighter or curvier, they should be going from the bushes to the goats' house, to the store, back to the goat's house, to the paint store, back to the goats' house, to the wolf's house, and finally to the water.

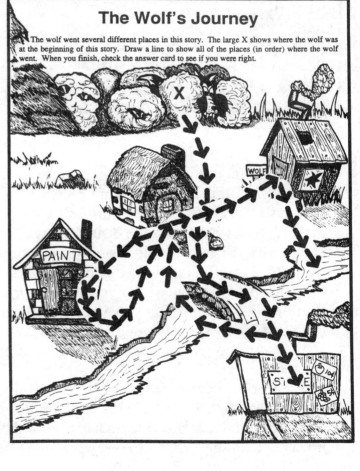

The Wolf's Journey

The wolf went several different places in this story. The large X shows where the wolf was at the beginning of this story. Draw a line to show all of the places (in order) where the wolf went. When you finish, check the answer card to see if you were right.

GA1144

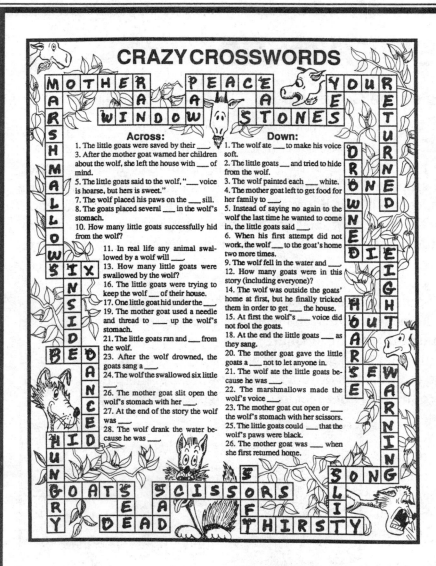

CRAZY CROSSWORDS

Across:
1. The little goats were saved by their ___.
3. After the mother goat warned her children about the wolf, she left the house with ___ of mind.
5. The little goats said to the wolf, "___ voice is hoarse, but hers is sweet."
7. The wolf placed his paws on the ___ sill.
8. The goats placed several ___ in the wolf's stomach.
10. How many little goats successfully hid from the wolf?
11. In real life any animal swallowed by a wolf will ___.
13. How many little goats were swallowed by the wolf?
16. The little goats were trying to keep the wolf ___ of their house.
17. One little goat hid under the ___.
19. The mother goat used a needle and thread to ___ up the wolf's stomach.
21. The little goats ran and ___ from the wolf.
23. After the wolf drowned, the goats sang a ___.
24. The wolf the swallowed six little ___.
26. The mother goat slit open the wolf's stomach with her ___.
27. At the end of the story the wolf was ___.
28. The wolf drank the water because he was ___.

Down:
1. The wolf ate ___ to make his voice soft.
2. The little goats ___ and tried to hide from the wolf.
3. The wolf painted each ___ white.
4. The mother goat left to get food for her family to ___.
5. Instead of saying no again to the wolf the last time he wanted to come in, the little goats said ___.
6. When his first attempt did not work, the wolf ___ to the goat's home two more times.
9. The wolf fell in the water and ___.
12. How many goats were in this story (including everyone)?
14. The wolf was outside the goats' home at first, but he finally tricked them in order to get ___ the house.
15. At first the wolf's ___ voice did not fool the goats.
18. At the end the little goats ___ as they sang.
20. The mother goat gave the little goats a ___ not to let anyone in.
21. The wolf ate the little goats because he was ___.
22. The marshmallows made the wolf's voice ___.
23. The mother goat cut open or ___ the wolf's stomach with her scissors.
25. The little goats could ___ that the wolf's paws were black.
26. The mother goat was ___ when she first returned home.

A Grave Matter

There are several different ways to say this lesson. Compare your answer with the thought reflected in the following message (the messages should be similar): A mother goat will protect her young and will get even with anyone who tries to dine on her children!

Wolves in Other Stories

A is the story "Little Red Riding Hood." The wolf is chased away by a hunter. **B** is "The Three Little Pigs." The wolf falls into a pot of boiling water. **C** is "Peter and the Wolf." The wolf is tied to a stick and carried around upside down by some huntsmen. **D** is the fable "The Boy Who Cried 'Wolf.'" In this fable the wolf wins out by getting to eat the sheep.

The Many Faces of the Wolf

1 is C; 2 is D; 3 is B; 4 is A.

The Old Goat and Wolf Talk

Many different stories may be created for each of these situations. Every story will be different. The following is one sample story for "Wolf Talk":

"I proved that I could outsmart the little goats. It was the old mother goat who got her revenge on me! Wolves would starve to death if they could not find anything to eat. And we do like to eat little goats! Since these little goats can be tricked, it is only the mother goat that we need to worry with. Therefore, I would like to give advice to other wolves who are hungry.

"My first piece of advice is for you not to return **home** after you eat the little goats. The mother goat will know where to find you and she will come after you. So after you eat the little goats, go to a place where she will not look for you.

"My next piece of advice is to stay awake after you eat the goats. If you are awake, you can see the mother goat when she is coming to get you—and she **will** come to get you. If you cannot stay awake, at least get a friend to stand guard for you. That friend can let you know if the enemy is approaching. (Maybe you should save a little goat for this friend to eat.)

"My final advice is never to underestimate the power of the old goat! She will do anything to protect her children. **Always** be aware of the fact that she will try to get you back!"

GA1144